Praise for *Shell-Shocked*

"*Shell-Shocked* is a must-read for anyone recovering from the disorientation and desensitization of the Trump years. Honig's feminist lens permits us to see past an overwhelming barrage of words, images, and video outtakes to reveal how patriarchy remains the foundation of so much of what ails us. Honig brings keen observation and wry humor to dazzling readings of literature, cinema, and cable news, as well as to the everyday moments that have troubled and confounded us. Her insights not only make us smarter; they promise to equip us for the work toward justice that lies ahead."
　　—Martha S. Jones, author of *Vanguard: How Black Women Broke Barriers, Won the Vote, and Insisted on Equality for All*

"Honig's book is precise because precision is what the technique of shock needs to exclude and negate. It is funny and ironic because irony is what white supremacist dogma cannot bear. It is dedicated to collective feminist action because neoliberalism simulates individualism and creates fearful isolation."
　　—Carolin Emcke, author of *How We Desire*

"A breath of fresh air. Honig's take on our current political scene is always illuminating but never despairing. *Shell-Shocked* is precisely what we need now to re-sensitize ourselves to the modes of anti-democratic and patriarchal power that shape our moment, without losing hope, creativity, or humor in how to fight for democratic action and equality."
　　—Elisabeth Anker, author of *Orgies of Feeling: Melodrama and the Politics of Freedom*

Shell-Shocked

FEMINIST CRITICISM AFTER TRUMP

Bonnie Honig

FORDHAM UNIVERSITY PRESS   NEW YORK 2021

Fordham University Press also publishes its books in a variety of electronic formats. Some content that appears in print may not be available in electronic books.

Visit us online at www.fordhampress.com.

Library of Congress Control Number: 2020925118

Printed in the United States of America

23 22 21   5 4 3 2 1

First edition

for Bruce Robbins

Contents

    in Portland   163

25 Impenetrable:
    Gaslighting the 14th Amendment   171

26 "Hallelujah": The People Want Their
    House Back   178

27 Loose Threads   184

    ACKNOWLEDGMENTS   195

    NOTES   199

    CREDITS   241

Therefore—we do life's labor—
Though life's Reward—be done—
With scrupulous exactness—
To hold our Senses—on—

—EMILY DICKINSON,
"I TIE MY HAT—I CREASE MY SHAWL—"

Let the world we dream about be the one
    we live in now!

—ORPHEUS, IN HADESTOWN

Preface

Trump will be gone by the time you are reading this book, but Trumpism will still be around in one form or another. Why am I so sure? Because like many things Trump, Trumpism is just a name slapped onto things that were already out there.

Trump gave a name to a toxic flambé of misogyny, xenophobia, and racism and then lit the flame. Together with a weakness for celebrity, these are America's "pre-existing conditions."

When Covid-19 hit some American communities especially hard in the first wave of 2020, the virus served as a barometer of inequality. The so-called co-morbidities of asthma, diabetes, and being overweight are often the results of one's living in toxic environments: food deserts with polluted air, poisoned water, and poor ventilation. The real pre-existing conditions here are racism and inequality, and they take their toll.

For Trump, Americans' asymmetrical vulnerability to the virus was not a condemnation of white supremacy but a vindication of it, further evidence that white people are biologically superior to those of other races. He attributed his own quick recovery from Covid not to the exceptional (publicly funded) care he received at Walter Reed Hospital but to his superior genetic endowments. His youngest son tested positive, too, but Barron, whose name was one of Trump's aliases in the 1980s, never got sick. Reporting on his son's seeming immunity, Trump proudly noted that his son was tall. That seemed strange, since the virus is indifferent to height. But this was Trump's way of celebrating genetic inheritance and taking credit for it. Why not? He had slapped his name on Barron too.

White supremacy kills. Minimizing the harms of the virus and touting white immunity to it cost hundreds of thousands of lives from every corner of American society. As one young woman put it, talking about her father who was lost to Covid, "his only pre-existing condition was believing in Donald Trump."

During the final weeks of his 2020 campaign for reelection, Trump accused doctors of inflating the number of Covid cases to make money. Shocked to be called profiteers when they had sacrificed so much, doctors turned "Dying not lying" into a hashtag and shared memoria of health workers who had lost their lives to the virus. Many had been let down by the social contract of care and concern and were left to repurpose garbage bags for protection in the absence of proper equipment that the federal government was slow to provide.

I write in the final hours before Joe Biden is named president-elect and Kamala Harris vice-president–elect. Now it is poll workers, counting the votes in the 2020 election, who are at risk, as they tabulate the count in several states. They are at risk not only from the virus, which continues to rage through the population, but also from Trumpism, which, raging through the body politic, feverishly foments conspiracies that send armed militia members and Boogaloo Boys to the counting places. One poll worker in Georgia had to go into hiding after being falsely accused of throwing out a ballot. The Republican City Commissioner of Philadelphia reported that his office was receiving death threats for counting votes. The lives of election workers are endangered when the idea of public service is discredited. Those who think poll workers are just in it for themselves find it easy to suspect they are up to no good. Like a virus, this cynicism about public service will seem to come and go in the coming years, sometimes spreading like wildfire, then embering and fooling us into thinking it has safely disappeared—like a miracle.

Trumpism, which this volume analyzes in a series of short essays written from 2016 to 2020, will have other names in the future, just as it has in the past, but what it names will not go gently into that good night. It names a kind of male entitlement for which it feels like freedom to just be able to say what you think and grab what you want. But freedom is not impulsiveness, and it cannot take root in division.

The opposite of impulsiveness is self-restraint. Some call that dignity, which is what Joe Biden said he wanted to bring back to Washington. Real freedom lies in lifting ourselves collectively to heights that were once unattainable. It is not about being superior to others, nor is it merely a matter of personal virtue. It is about uniting because there is strength in numbers and power in union. And the affect of freedom is not rage; it is joy, which is what Kamala Harris said she wants to bring back to Washington.

The affect of the Trump presidency was not joy but shock. Shell shock was the deliberate result of the constant tweeting, daily controversies, and calls for investigations, all of which contributed to a four-year-long ambient rumble of rage, gaslighting, and resentment. Public norms and institutions, which had been tested and violated before, were now openly dismantled and commandeered to avoid accountability.

The power of shock is in its seeming implacability. Shock overwhelms a people's senses; it breaks apart individuals, communities, and institutions; and it paralyzes us. Flooding the airwaves with lies presented as alternative facts, shock attenuates the practice of public deliberation and destroys the quiet of critical reflection. It is disorienting. Instead of walking with purpose, we find ourselves stumbling.

I argue in this collection that the kind of attention to detail practiced by feminist criticism can help us find patterns in the chaos of shock and points of orientation in the miasma. Close reading helps loosen the grip of shock or at least prevent its further tightening. It brings discernment to the disarray. Criticism brings us together to share impressions, develop collaborations, and compare perspectives. Feminist criticism tears at the fabric of America's pre-existing conditions and loosens its binds.

Then, one day the grip of shock is broken, and joy marks the moment and helps reset our bearings. It happens not like a miracle, but like the product of years-long hard work, much of it done by Black women, union members, the Latinx community, and groups like Indivisible and others in whose names chapters were set up all over the country. For months or years, people woke up every day to register voters, empower people, fight suppression, overcome division, organize communities, encourage dance at protests, and play music outside election halls. Seeing to the details and committing to the everyday, these actions created a public united against America's divisions. They gave life to the public option: a kind of collective insurance that commits each to all in times of hardship and leaves no one behind because of their so-called pre-existing conditions.

And then, the count is complete, and the shock that once seemed implacable is replaced by implacable procedure, the seemingly unstoppable machinery of the peaceful transfer of power. At other times in other moments, that machinery overwhelmed the will of the people. But not this time. Just now, as I continue to write, the election is called for Biden–Harris, and thousands and thousands of people everywhere have gathered spontaneously in the streets, joined in joy on an implausibly beautiful and sunny November day. We are plural, we are often disagreeable, but today, anyway, many of us are dancing in the public streets. There is still so much work to do, but no one is gassing or brutalizing the people today and the view from here is almost fine.

Bonnie Honig
Warren, VT
Nov. 7, 2020

1
Trump's Family Romance and the Magic of Television

[He] is nothing if not a televisual thinker.
—JAMES PONIEWOZIK

In *The Art of the Deal*, Trump recalls the day of Elizabeth II's coronation, which, in his telling, becomes a kind of televisual primal scene. Trump was seven years old at the time. Recalling it over thirty years later, he says:

> I still remember my mother, who is Scottish by birth, sitting in front of the television set to watch Queen Elizabeth's coronation and not budging for an entire day. She was enthralled by the pomp and circumstance, the whole idea of royalty and glamour. I also remember my father that day, pacing around impatiently. "For Christ's sake, Mary," he'd say. "Enough is enough, turn it off. They're all a bunch of con artists." My mother didn't even look up.[1]

Trump tells the story to account for his love of pageantry, which he claims he inherited from his mother. It is from her,

not from his practical father, that he learns to gild the surfaces of his properties, he says. His way of telling the story
suggests he identified with his mother's refusal to yield
that day to his father. But the story relates something else,
too: the moment Trump imprinted on TV, which was the
source of his mother's power that day, and with what
consequences.

One obvious consequence is that Trump became a TV
celebrity forty years later, and by then TV, which had been
in its infancy in 1953, was all grown up. It became Trump's
standard of measure. For him, success in that medium is
success as such, as he made clear when he mocked the TV
ratings of Arnold Schwarzenegger, his successor on *The
Celebrity Apprentice*, and gloated that Robert Mueller's less
than telegenic appearance before the House in 2019 was
reason enough to nullify his entire report.[2]

But television is not just a yardstick for Trump. The story
in *The Art of the Deal* suggests a deeper attachment, evidenced later by his behavior in public office. Over sixty years
after Elizabeth's coronation, he is president, and he spends
hours every morning watching television. Is it because he
loves the news? Yes, the Fox Channel version. Is he just
keeping track of his numbers? Assessing the coverage of him
and his followers? Yes, that too. But he is also in a way spend-
ing the morning with his mother, or so his childhood story
of the 1953 coronation suggests. For Trump, TV is a site of
maternal attachment, dating back to the day his long-
suffering mother took time to watch a royal coronation on
TV and was emboldened for once to refuse to yield to her
browbeating husband.[3]

Trump's mother expressed no anger that day; she did not
even look up then, keeping her eyes on the TV screen. But
Trump's TV-watching now is accompanied by rage. Why?
While commentators try to explain his temper tweets with

reference to specific stories being broadcast on Fox, the rage often exceeds any such content. What may explain it is this: if television is a site of maternal attachment for Trump, then watching it reenters him also into his father's abusive dismissal: "For Christ's sake!"

The story told in *The Art of the Deal* is not only primal scene, however: it is also family romance. In the Freudian family romance, a young child of about Trump's age at the time fantasizes that the drab people he lives with are not his real parents and that his real parents are rich and important, royals or nobles who are surely still looking for him.[4] In Trump's version of the Freudian fantasy, which is televisual, his mother does not simply watch Elizabeth get crowned on TV. In the watching, and in his watching her watching, Trump's *mother in Queens becomes his mother, the queen!*

This is the real magic of television for Trump: it exposes the dingy life of a browbeaten housewife and her browbeaten son as a terrible mistake, it transfers his Scottish mother's maternity to the queen and this remakes Trump into the lost offspring of a royal.[5] The fantasy validates the child's grandiosity and corrects the terrible injustice of his obscurity as *Elizabeth's coronation becomes virtually his.*

But what happens, psychologically, when the Queens housewife becomes the English queen? Does that miracle free the son of paternal judgment or freeze him further into it? "Enough is enough," Trump recalls his father saying that day. For the younger Trump, therefore, enough is *never* enough: excess will later be his trademark. Trump will brush off the bankruptcies, and, when he fails as a businessman, he will play one on TV. But he is frozen into his father's judgment nonetheless. If "they"—the royals—are all "a bunch of con artists," then so too will be their long-lost son: Trump. Apple, meet tree.

This means that when, during the 2019 House impeachment hearings, the Stanford constitutional law scholar
Pamela Karlan made light of the fact that Trump named his
son with a word that is also a royal title, she lit on a detail that
mattered. Like a loose thread when pulled on, that detail
helps to unravel a larger fabric.

> "Contrary to what President Trump says, Article Two
> [of the Constitution] does not give him the power to
> do anything he wants," Karlan said. "And I'll just give
> you one example that shows you the difference
> between him and a king, which is the Constitution
> says there can be no titles of nobility, so while the
> president can name his son Barron, he cannot make
> him a baron."[6]

The son, Barron, was by then thirteen, much older than
seven, the age of his father in 1953 when the seed of the
child's name was planted by the coronation of the queen,
(as) his mother. But, at the age of thirteen, the son was still
a child all the same, and Karlan was criticized for what
Republicans claimed was her outrageous violation of an
innocent. Although other actual innocent children at that
moment were being held captive in camps at the U.S./
Mexico border, Karlan apologized. But for what, exactly?
Saying his name?

Karlan's target was not the child but the father, who chose
a name for his son that had actually been one of his own.
Barron was Trump's longtime alias, starting in the 1980s,
when he disguised his voice and posed on the telephone as
John Barron, his own spokesman, to manage press coverage
of his activities. Remarkably, it worked.[7] Today's outrage at
Karlan's name-saying achieves what Trump's use of the
name did then. Deflection, now, and deception, then: both
block further inquiry.

A few months after the impeachment hearings, on Twitter on March 28, 2020, Daniel Drezner referred to Karlan's reference to the son as an "offhand mention," meaning to note how manufactured was the outrage that followed it. It was manufactured, he was right.[8] But it is also a thread worth pulling on. When Trump named his child Barron, he was living out his family romance; unable to make the child a baron, he could nonetheless ennoble him with the name. But it is not just that. The name is a loose thread in the politics of America's romance with celebrity and flirtation with royalty, an expression of many Americans' fundamental longing to crown their presidents and let them be royals.

When in April 2020 Trump persistently misspelled on Twitter the name Nobel—as in Nobel Prize—as Noble, he was mocked for the error (he was meaning to talk about Pulitzer Prizes) and for the misspelling, but no one picked up on the loose thread here: his penchant for nobility. Nor was the irony later noted when he was sickened by Covid-19 that this was a *corona* virus and his illness, therefore, the dark double of the coronation he had long sought.

America's royalism was noted by Thomas Jefferson, who said the Constitution "wears a mixed aspect of monarchy and republicanism." He neglected the despotism that was also constitutionally entrenched in the 3/5 clause of the Constitution.[9] The result was a mix of monarchy and republicanism, with a big dash of tyranny, that still makes mischief and misery in American political culture, from Kennedy's Camelot to Trump's daily performance of *l'état c'est moi* (in which he decries the "terrible things done to our country," by which he means himself), to the "overpolicing" and criminalization of people of color.[10] The personal yearning by some Americans to rule monarchically and the political yearning by many to be so ruled, even as many others, still somehow scenting in the political fabric the faint fragrance of freedom and equality, strive ever more determinedly toward them—these make up the rhythm and rhyme of American political culture.

The hope of Jefferson was that the spirit of republicanism would triumph over the constitutionally entrenched relic of the monarchical form; others hoped despotism, too, might be similarly vanquished. Instead, in the twentieth and twenty-first centuries, the power of the federal government's legislative branch has been diminished and the executive increased by a series of emergencies (Depression, WWII, 9/11) and, since 2017, by a president who would be king and who has gone out of his way to feminize the legislative branch, especially the House, whose speaker, since 2018, he calls Nervous Nancy, though we have never seen her nervous.[11] Jefferson and others saw the representative and participatory virtues of republicanism as *manly,* so they might have been especially alarmed by the feminization of the legislative branch (though of course they would have been surprised, even appalled, to find a woman serving as speaker; but that is not the only detail of the moment that would appall them, surely). Pamela Karlan's attempted witticism at the impeachment hearing stumbled on all of this. And that makes her little joke an act of feminist criticism.

Feminist criticism is different from feminist theory.[12] Where feminist theory aims to be systematic, feminist criticism is more nimble and more pointed. Where the horizon of feminist theory is remote and its apparatus weighty, feminist criticism works from the particular to the general, not the other way round. Feminist criticism is oriented to the time of now while connecting to larger patterns, contexts, and timelines. It proceeds by observation and offers readings of texts or events, not articulations of principles or deductions of norms, though its readings are compassed by feminist theory's normativity.

Both feminist theory and criticism document gender inequalities in the hope of correcting them, and both move beyond feminism's main goal—to empower women—in order to attend more broadly to *feminization*. Feminization is the complex array of discourses and practices that reproduce, secure, and advance hierarchical divisions of sexuality, gender, race, ability, indigeneity, ethnicity, lineage, and class that make the world legible, hospitable, and accessible to some more than others. Feminization is a device of disorientation and a practice of desensitization. It works at a sensorial level by demeaning and degrading whole swaths of populations, outlooks, and behaviors, demanding their submission, compliance, or silence, and exhorting others to join the circle of bullying. Feminist criticism has its own unique way of responding to feminization, which is pressed daily into the service of a kind of shock politics. The task of feminist criticism, and this is what makes it particularly well suited to the moment, is to sensitize the senses and hone the empathy needed for living with others in the world as equals. Its penchant for the particular is part of its power. It focuses our attention on the individual and the idiosyncratic. It is drawn to the loose threads of psychological and collective life, not to the well-worn fabrics or fabrications in which nations are wrapped to hide their shortcomings and deflect critical scrutiny.

Naomi Klein's *The Shock Doctrine* (2007) gives us the best account of shock politics we have, connecting it to what she calls "disaster capitalism," but she does not consider shock's longstanding partnership with misogyny.[13] A specifically feminist analysis of shock remains to be done. That work could be done as theory or as criticism. I choose the latter in this collection because I believe in the importance now of the grounding power of close reading and the wild connections of loosened threads to offset the shock politics program of disorientation and desensitization. The hope is that grounding counters disorientation, that wild connections resensitize the senses, and that, together, they help energize a joyful citizenship that refocuses attention on the urgent tasks at hand.

Exhaustion is a feature of shock politics, the deliberate product of disinformation. In the last twenty years, subjected to (dis)information overload under both Bush II (shock and awe) and Trump (who you gonna believe?) Republicanism, we have become enmeshed in a shock politics of disinformation that disorients and destabilizes democratic institutions, practices, and habits, aggravating inequalities of all sorts. Shock now is the impact on citizens of living in a world in which the real and the fake, the authentic and corrupt, the public-minded and the self-serving can be hard to distinguish, and disorientation rules. Deprived of once reliable— not necessarily indisputable or incontestable, but reliable—points of orientation, like news reporting or CDC guidance, and saturated by noise and accusations every day at every minute, people are thrown back onto themselves, and the result is, at best, solipsistic confusion and, at worst, destructive conspiracy-thinking and paranoid politics. Worse yet, the disorientating powers of shock make (trans) national publics vulnerable not only to the predatory privat-izations of Klein's disaster capitalism but also (as she herself notes) to the routine corruptions of would-be oligarchs.

Trump himself has long been a practiced purveyor of shock. Here is his rather pithy statement of his version of the shock doctrine: "'You know what solves it?' Trump said of America's alleged troubles during a 2014 interview. 'When the economy crashes, when the country goes to total hell and everything is a disaster. Then you'll have a [chuckles], you know, you'll have riots to go back to where we used to be when we were great.'"[14] There is something going on in that chuckle, which is humorless. It is a distancing technique. And "you'll have riots" means "I will watch them on my TV in my tower." (Or, as in June 2020, in the PEOC, the presi-dent's emergency bunker in the White House, as occurred during the protests of the police killing of George Floyd.) And "total hell" is the prelude to what Naomi Klein calls the tabula rasa, the clean canvas on which disaster capitalism wants to paint our future. Trump, a brass-knuckled New York City developer, several times bankrupted before he became a reality TV personality and then a reality TV pres-ident, perfectly embodies the blend of thuggery, grift, irre-sponsibility, and chaos that *is* shock politics.[15]

He is also famously thin-skinned, with no sense of humor, it is said. This brings me to the last feature of feminist criti-cism: its enlistment of humor to crack the surface of the serious. Walter Benjamin noted nearly a century ago that laughter enables thinking by rendering the familiar strange.[16] Nowadays, however, our task may be a bit different: to find in the strange something familiar by way of which to orient ourselves and to relieve the exhaustion of the moment by generating through laughter the energy and insight we need to combat shock politics.

If Pamela Karlan's joke about Barron/baron caused such consternation, it is because *she did not just call the son by his name, she named us by her call*: a call to engage civically as democratic citizens against the royal privilege of self-exemption while doing the work of constant interpretation, repair, and vigilance that are the mainstays of feminist criticism *and* democratic citizenship. This is the legacy left to a once slaveholding country that entrenched monarchy/patriarchy at the center of a republican constitution designed to take the place of a once supposedly rightful monarch.

Of course, the fraught focus in December 2019 on the named son distracted attention from the Cassandra-like truths uttered by Karlan at the time in her effort to make totally clear during the impeachment hearings the problem with permitting an American president to extract a quid pro quo from Ukraine under duress: "What would you think if, when your [state] governor asked the federal government for the disaster assistance that Congress has provided, the President responded, 'I would like you to do us a favor. I'll . . . send the disaster relief once you brand my opponent a criminal.'"[17]

As we learned just three to four months later, in the spring of the 2020 coronavirus pandemic, this was no crazy hypothetical. He might extort a different quid pro quo from state governors, but a quid pro quo it was, all the same. Instead of asking for dirt on an opponent, he might say, your ventilators will arrive when you learn to say thank you and stop criticizing the president in public. Show some gratitude: "All I want them to do, very simple, I want them to be appreciative. I don't want them to say things that aren't true. I want them to be appreciative. We've done a great job." In March 2020, Trump said about Governor Cuomo, at that moment struggling from behind, finally, to prepare New York State for a vast public health emergency, "It's a two-way street, they have to treat us well also." About all the governors working with the federal government to prepare, he said, "If they don't treat you right, I don't call."[18]

This is not just Trump's much-vaunted transactionalism. Feminist criticism sees it more clearly: it is a move in the game of patriarchal domination, in which it is no surprise that a female governor loses her name: "We've had a big problem with the young, a woman governor from, you know who I'm talking about, from Michigan," as if saying Governor Whitmer's name might grant her dignity or agency. It might.[19]

On behalf of their constituents, some of the governors submitted, a bit like feudal lords to a king bent on usurping their independence. They offered up some positive-sounding things about the president or the federal government as they scrambled in a still open and competitive marketplace, often forced to bid against each other, and even against the feds, to acquire much needed ventilators, masks, gloves, and gowns for their essential workers. Governors Cuomo (New York) and Newsom (California) were the first to oblige. Their words, just some of their words, were immediately harvested for a TV ad promoting the president.[20]

It is hard not to think this was the purpose all along, to extract praise to be used as "content" for marketing purposes. This is what the public relations people of rapists and harassers do when queried about accusations, and it is what their lawyers do in court: offer up any seemingly friendly text or apparently genial conduct later by the victim as evidence that coercion did not occur when in fact it is just as likely evidence it did. And is still. The tactic has often worked in the past. Ask Harvey Weinstein. But it may not always do so

in the future. Ask the brave women of the #MeToo movement, who wove together the tattered threads of their experiences and made a social movement out of them.

The practice of feminist criticism takes inspiration from
these and many other women, real and fictional. My favorite
in the latter group is Homer's Penelope, who knows all about
tattered threads. In the *Odyssey*, as Penelope waits and waits
for Odysseus's return, she weaves a shroud by day and unrav-
els it nightly. Unraveling means finding a loose thread and
pulling on it until the fabric comes undone. That requires a
certain attention to detail. In a way, this book is a collection
of loose threads that I have drawn out of the tight fabrics of
shock politics' practices of social domination. The hope is to
contribute to a great unraveling. When we are made to
doubt our senses, feminist criticism recommits to them,
with doubled focus and renewed attention to detail. Penelope
unraveled her fabric for years, every night, in a bid to preserve her independence. Her indefatigability is another of
the traits that make her an important model for feminist
criticism now. Later in this volume I will suggest that we see
her, anachronistically, as the first in a long line of gothic
heroines, shut up in castles, country retreats, aristocratic
manors, beautiful houses, or terrible rooms, isolated from
others and left with only their wits and intelligence to save
them from men who might be monsters. Then as now, the
monsters of the moment are not extraordinary men, just
those privileged enough that they are accustomed to having
their say and doing their thing, and all of them well-practiced
in the politics of shock.

2

Gaslight and the Shock Politics Two-Step

a kind of hurricane in the mind

—NAOMI KLEIN

What happens when we think of shock not just in connection with disaster capitalism but also with disaster patriarchy?

Shock politics means those empowered by the current political moment work to deprive the public of fixed or stable points of orientation and then flood the public's senses with stimuli such that we are overwhelmed, desensitized, and disoriented, left nearly incapable of response or action because we are confused, exhausted, or fatigued, rather like the U.S. and Canadian diplomats in Cuba who were made ill by some mysterious, silent assault on the senses. Shock calls attention to this specifically sensorial precarity. For the last two-and-a-half decades, scholars studied precarity as an effect of working conditions and material inequality. Both precarities are disorienting, but the sensorial one has impacts that are heightened by disinformation, bot, and corporate mediation, and it not only exploits labor ever more fully but also deactivates citizenship ever more completely.

The combination of disorientation and desensitization that I call the shock politics two-step is a two-part assault on the senses, consisting in sensory deprivation followed by sensory saturation. Together these cause disorientation, disaffection, and alienation, civic fatigue, and, often, surrender. The two-step is in play throughout Naomi Klein's *The Shock Doctrine*, where the targets of shock are whole countries, states, or cities that have just experienced a disaster, natural or manmade, like a tsunami (Thailand), flood (New Orleans), military coup (Chile), or, since the publication of *The Shock Doctrine*, a new coronavirus (New York, then Florida, then Texas . . .).[1] Such disasters, which disorient most people on the ground, look like an opportunity to "disaster capitalists" who come in to rebuild and resegregate, by race or class, in pursuit of a locally unpopular but profitable neoliberal agenda of privatization and gentrification that destroys local infrastructures, loots domestic economies, and is often secured, in the face of resistance, by military power and the use of torture. In the words of Thai survivors of the 2004 Asian tsunami, to "businessmen-politicians, the tsunami was the answer to their prayers, since it literally wiped these coastal areas clean of the communities which had previously stood in the way of their plans for resorts, hotels, casinos and shrimp farms. To them, all these coastal areas are now" not the homes of bereft locals needing to rebuild, but "open land."[2] This is what Klein calls the tabula rasa strategy. It wipes clean the slate of land and history and deprives communities of shared points of orientation. Klein connects it to the use of electroshock therapy earlier in the twentieth century, specifically to U.S.-funded research by Ewen Cameron at McGill University, which used shock to wipe clean the slate of patients' minds.[3] The hope then was that their personalities could be depatterned, and this would rid them of undesirable habits, leaving a tabula rasa on which to inscribe good ones instead, through repetition and training.[4] In many cases, the result of these shock therapy experiments was lifelong suffering. Suffering follows the political use of shock, too.

The shock two-step recurs in all of Klein's examples. In the wake of disaster, blackouts and severed communications cause sensory *deprivation*.[5] Then sensory *saturation* is inflicted. This can be achieved via constant barrages of disinformation, what Steve Bannon calls "flooding the zone" (and of course floods are one of the natural disasters that make the shock two-step possible).[6] The same pattern characterizes the torture used in support of shock, as in the case, for example, of the U.S. in Iraq: first, deprivation—detainees hooded for days without access to light—and then, saturation—detainees, unhooded and subjected to nonstop bright lighting in their cells, again for days.[7]

What *The Shock Doctrine* does not mention is how shock is also characteristic of what has come to be called gaslighting. First, the woman being terrorized is isolated, deprived of normal social stimuli, public things, and activities, and of the company of others whose senses can confirm her experiences of hers. Then, disoriented, she is saturated by a flood of misinformation and false cues, until she comes to doubt her own mind and abilities. This shock two-step of deprivation and saturation is familiar to feminists who study the (in) delicacies of patriarchal degradation and to those who study the details of domination in the context of U.S. white supremacy. Denying the existence of structural misogyny and racism (Americans all have equal opportunity!) puts those who suffer from them in the position of trying to articulate experiences for which there are no words, because they are not allowed. Hence the creative response of the gaslit by way of terms like "double consciousness," "the veil," white "dreamers," and "consciousness raising." All try to give voice to experiences officially denied.

Hence too feminists' quick recognition of the shock tactics used by Trump, as for example when, six months into his term, in a meeting with military and political advisors, he said, "I wouldn't go to war with you people" and "You're a bunch of dopes and babies."[8] The use of humiliation, infantilization, and feminization to dominate is a common feature of domestic abuse. In paranoid gothic films like *Gaslight*, as in female gothic novels, the scene where the husband suddenly insults his new bride is the tip-off that the marriage will not be as expected.

George Cukor's *Gaslight* (1944), a paranoid gothic film with a noir aesthetic, depicts the household variety of shock and assigns responsibility for it to a single villain: the foreign, somewhat sexually ambiguous, and, finally, feminized Gregory Anton (Charles Boyer) who isolates his bride, Paula (Ingrid Bergman), and ruptures her connections with the larger social world in the hope of stealing her hidden treasure.[9] Made during WWII, *Gaslight*, set in England and (briefly) Italy, tells the story of how Paula is driven nearly mad by her husband, until a stranger intervenes on her behalf. *Gaslight* illustrates the vulnerability of the isolated individual to the machinations of the powerful. Anton begins by never leaving Paula alone. When he proposes marriage and she says she needs time to think about it, he feigns acceptance but secretly contrives to meet her train at her resort destination. Surprising her, he claims he just couldn't wait, and she yields to him, mistaking his attentions for true love. They marry immediately. This is his pattern: to deprive her of the kind of solitude that thinking requires and of the plurality without which perspective soon wilts. The love that allows for no time alone will soon become the loveless isolation of being alone all the time.

It is worth noting the comparison to Trump. He does not take a train to block our quest for solitude, but his constant tweeting has the same effect: it diminishes the space of refuge and shuts out the time of reflection. We are rarely alone with our own minds, always pressed into his company. While others see the constant tweeting as an expression of the man's narcissistic need to always be in the spotlight (which it may well be), *Gaslight* helps us see how it works as a *device of disorientation*, blocking access to the solitude and plurality that are the conditions of critical thinking and reflection.

Once Gregory and Paula are married, they move at his request to her childhood home in London. He does not share the real reason for the move: his interest is in some long-lost jewels he thinks are hidden there. In London, Gregory is able to gather a whole household to his purpose, an old trusted housekeeper and a new untrustworthy maid, and this helps him isolate Paula from friends and neighbors. He determinedly undermines Paula's faith in her own senses, claiming she has lost or stolen things he has moved or hidden. Gregory wants to distract her from his criminal activities. (Sound familiar? It should: the husband is a certain president and the country is the wife.) Gregory lies about little things to confuse Paula, flirts with the maid in Paula's presence to demean her, and isolates Paula from society. (American isolationism takes on a new meaning in this context. It is a way to insulate the American public from rival opinions and plural points of view.) Paula is a capable but traumatized person: years earlier, as an orphaned child living with her aunt, she stumbled on the scene of her aunt's murder. She is vulnerable to Gregory's machinations and is soon lost, doubting what she knows and blindly looking for a way to make sense of what is happening around her.

Isolated in the house, Paula becomes almost a recluse. Recall how the female gothic novel *Jane Eyre* begins with the line "There was no possibility of taking a walk that day." The reason is the rainy weather; but the confinement caused by the rain is a symbol of sorts for the movement-limiting strictures that Jane must break out of if she is to be a free and independent woman. In *Gaslight*, Paula is confined, too, but the weather is fine. Nonetheless, she cannot go out for a walk. She dresses, starts toward the door, even crosses the threshold to a gorgeous sunny day, but then the compromised maid asks: is the lady sure she wants to go out, and what should she tell the master if he asks? And Paula hesitates, then goes inside, reeled right back in by the uncertain weather of a man's mood.[10]

In the end, after a long intensifying period of confusion and terror, Paula finds a way out. She has lasted as long as she has, still sane but wavering, by clinging to one thing: the gaslight. In American political culture, "gaslight" is the word for male manipulation in the shock two-step of patriarchy. But in the film, gaslight is also the thread of Paula's salvation. It is the particular, singular material detail to which she clings as a port in the storm of Gregory's domination.[11]

In the evenings, when her husband claims to be out, strange things happen in the house, and they disturb Paula. Are they sounds and signs of some unworldly presence? Gregory is actually secretly rummaging in the attic looking for the jewels he plans to steal. (That is, instead of *Jane Eyre*'s husband with a secret in the attic, in *Gaslight* the husband *is* the secret in the attic.) When Gregory turns on the attic gaslights upstairs, the gas in the main floors' lights goes down, and Paula notices but can't explain it. If the gas goes up and down, why should that be? Surely it means

something. She clings to this detail as a fact, though she cannot be sure of it, and she doesn't know what to make of it.

John Locke (who *assumes* the tabula rasa—the blank slate—that Naomi Klein says practitioners of shock therapy and politics try to *create*) instructs us in his *Essay on Human Understanding* to limit our sensory apprehension to our own senses, to rely only on their "proper inlets" to take in the

world and not to claim to see, hear, or know things we have
not directly experienced through direct sensory apprehension. Such self-discipline can vouchsafe certain knowledge,
he says, and fend off confusion.[12] He assumes things are
what they are and are what they seem, but this is something
women and minorities cannot safely assume. Thus, when
Locke warns against nursemaids who infect their charges'
upper-class minds with stories of ghosts and fancies, he does
not stop to ask why lower-class women might tell such stories
or why children might be drawn to them. Both are subject
to powers that move over them, often in mysterious ways,
but Locke neutralizes the knowledge of the nursery. It is a
gothic moment in his philosophical text.

In *Gaslight*, and in paranoid gothic films more generally,
women's direct experience confuses and does not orient.[13]
That is because the women are deprived of the *common*
sense that Locke failed to note is necessary to our capacity
to sense at all. Perhaps he failed to note it because he could
take it for granted. Hannah Arendt notes it, though. It is
actually, she says, "by virtue of common sense that the other
sense perceptions are known to disclose reality and are not
merely felt as irritations of our nerves or resistance sensa-
tions of our bodies."[14] The *common sense*—which is a kind
of extrasensory perception, a sixth sense—is the underwrit-
ing power of all the senses. Without "common sense" we
might twitch but we would not feel or know. Arendt did not
have today's media in mind, but nonetheless she provides
the beginning of a critique of them for generating in us a
certain twitchiness.[15] (I think here of how one streaming
platform is called Twitch.)

Locke's empiricism can't save Paula because she is made
to doubt the evidence of her senses, and Arendt cannot help
her, either, because although Paula continually seeks, she
cannot find the *common* that sensory apprehension requires.

She yearns to attend social gatherings to gauge the shared world in common with others and to be seen by others in ways that are different from how her husband sees her. But Gregory tells her she is too ill to go out. She checks with her longtime housekeeper, seeking to make common her sense that the gas in the lamplights is going up and down in the evenings. But the housekeeper says honestly that she has not noticed any change in lighting. She is an older woman, hard of hearing and apparently not sensitive to other sensory stimuli, either. In any case, she is not inclined to take Paula's observations too seriously because Gregory has told her that Paula is ill and that her senses cannot be trusted.

The other woman in the household, younger than Paula (Angela Lansbury in her first film role) and hired by Gregory without consulting his wife and over her objections, is enlisted by Gregory to become part of the plot.[16] When he flirts with the maid, he encourages her ill-mannered behavior with both his wife and the housekeeper. Through a kind of pretense of social egalitarianism that interests him not at all (accompanied by moments of *noblesse* but not *oblige*, during which he instructs Paula to command the servants more assertively), Gregory divides the women, positions Paula as unreliable, and makes himself head of the household he has married into and full owner of the property— Paula's house—that is now his.[17]

When Gregory makes things disappear and blames Paula for their loss, he manipulates her psychologically, but he also performs in a gothic register the conventional legal script of marriage in which things that were once a woman's become her husband's to manage as he likes without her knowledge or consent.[18] The film personalizes what the law does as a matter of course and structure. When Gregory talks to Paula pityingly and she comes to think she is pitiable, we see in compressed time how marriage in patriarchy can deconstruct and disorient a woman over a life. Paula seems bound for an insane asylum, which is Gregory's deep desire: with her gone, he could search more freely for the jewels he craves but that so far elude him. Importantly, driving her insane is not just his criminal aim in a plot against her; it is also a structural dimension of ordinary marriage, to which some women nonetheless adapt well, or well enough, but others, who do not, suffer.

Paula is rescued. A Scotland Yard inspector, Brian Cameron (played by Joseph Cotten), finds a way into her house, where she is secluded. He has grown suspicious of her situation. Years earlier, as a boy, he met her aunt, Alice Alquist, a famous opera singer he admired. Alquist was murdered soon after and the case never solved. Cameron is struck by the physical resemblance between Alquist and the anxious young woman he has seen around London. When he finds out that Paula is actually Alquist's niece, he wants to help. Paula is slow to trust him until Cameron shares with her his innocent admiration, as a boy of twelve, for her aunt, the opera star. He has brought proof: a glove once given to him by Paula's aunt as a souvenir at a concert. Will it match an orphaned one left behind and now in her niece's possession in a display case? Paula compares the gloves, and they match. Like the slipper in *Cinderella*, here too a pair of *things* reunited will remake the world.

Other *things* follow suit: a letter whose existence Gregory had denied is found in the desk Cameron dares to rummage through. Paula recognizes the letter. She had thought it was a clue to solving her aunt's murder, but Gregory hid it away and told her it was a figment of her imagination. Cameron shows her that the letter, which is signed by a man of another name, is written in handwriting that matches Gregory's, and now Paula can no longer doubt the evidence of her senses. Gregory is not who he says he is. All the fabrications and secrets that imprisoned her start to unravel, and Paula's disorientation gives way to a worldly reorientation, confirmed in the company of another person and engineered by worldly things: an errant glove returned, the materiality of the letter, the matched handwriting, sounds from the attic, and the changing gaslight.

When the sounds now come from the attic, and the gaslight flickers, Paula is offered the further salvation of observing Cameron noticing the sights and sounds, too. Cameron follows the sensory clues and ascends to catch Gregory in the act of stealing the aunt's missing jewels, which he has finally found. Cameron ties Gregory up in the attic, and Paula—newly confident of her own sanity—goes up to confront her now impotent husband. All along calling to mind Bruno, Hitchcock's gay, obsessive villain in the later film *Strangers on a Train* (1951), Gregory is now even more openly feminized than before, and he confesses to Paula the obsession for which he betrayed her. He could not control his desire for the jewels, he explains, as he moves from domination to dependence, from an appearance of rational calm to uncontrolled feminized obsession. He tries to wheedle Paula into freeing him, and she toys with him, pretending to consider it. He falls for her feigning as she fell for his. The irony surely is that he had planned to turn Paula into the proverbial madwoman in the attic, and that has now become his fate, not hers. Gregory is arrested. Here we see how the law occludes its structural misogyny, which empowers men over women, by once in a while saving a good woman from an occasional bad man.

But what frees Paula, more fundamentally, is Cameron's faith in the power of facts and in a facticity that depends upon and secures shared experience among plural others.[19] Cameron seems to understand the need to provide Paula with a source of epistemic certainty to break the spell of

Anton's mesmerism. Locke's empiricism flexes its muscles here, but we see how Arendt's common sense is also necessary, and it is that which was denied to Paula, in isolation.

In the end, the film may seem to have a rather naive faith in the power of the true to triumph over the false. After all, for us, in today's online world, reality is manipulated not by just one man, bubbles of isolation are much harder to burst, and handwriting's giveaway is almost a thing of the past (though digital markers do leave behind "fingerprints"). Ascertaining the truth or falsity of online claims means we must distinguish the Brian Camerons from the shock doctors like Klein's Ewen Cameron and from the Gregory Antons in an arena where individual agency defies location even by the most powerful discernments. Or we may dispense with such men entirely and follow our own lights, even though, in so doing, we risk slipping into the individualism of the U.S. where we live by the rule of *caveat emptor* and make truth into a product we may choose to buy, or not, with the decision being a matter of everyone's individual responsibility. "Make up your own mind!" and "I don't buy it" are familiar phrases for this reason.

But *Gaslight* gets one thing quite right. Truth is in trouble against domination. Truth requires an infrastructure, and popular subscription to it is one of truth's essential features. Truth cannot survive in isolation, not for long. It depends on the corroboration of others—what Hannah Arendt called "plurality" (hence we sometimes ask, "Do you see what I see?")—and on the facticity of material evidence. It depends on public things and institutions, including those that claim truth as their foundation. Here the curious American phrase "we hold these truths to be self-evident" perfectly captures the situation. If the truths we live by are self-evident, why do *we* have to hold *them*? Don't they hold us?[20] Yes, but we have to hold them, too, or they may give way. A chair holds us, but if we allow it to fall into disrepair, it may one day collapse and land us with a hard thud on the hard floor.[21]

Holding the truth now means rebutting false claims of disinformation, but such rebuttals also energize false claims, increasing the life of their news cycle, widening their impact, and contributing further to a sense of helplessness and civic exhaustion. The heroines of female gothics and paranoid gothic film are helpful here, since they too are plagued by helplessness and exhaustion. Now, in the context of the post-9/11 American shock politics of the twenty-first century, gothic women's exemplary return to feeling and sensation is instructive. *Gaslight*, in particular, is instructive because it does not just document the infliction of sensory degradation on a woman by a domineering man.[22] It is also about her return to her senses. This is what the changing gaslight represents. She sees the lighting change, and, her sensory confusion notwithstanding, she clings to that fact and will not let it go. That is why she can be summoned back to the shared world. In the face of deprivation and disorientation, she never let it go.

We see something similar in the television streaming series *Stranger Things*. In Season 1, Joyce Byers's son Will is missing.[23] The boy is trapped in a parallel world, but she does not know that yet. She just knows he is gone. She notices lights turning on and off in her house. Everyone else (the sheriff, her older son) says it is a "power surge," but Joyce, like Paula in *Gaslight*, tunes *in* to the light. Joyce, who has suffered (poverty, divorce), is not subjected to deliberate sensory deprivation. No one has been working full time to make her doubt herself. Still, it is remarkable that she can trust her senses in the absence of sensorial sharedness. She is a singular character, bound and determined, not deterred by others' doubts. It helps that she is a little bit mad or quirky, plucky in the way some small-town poor people are depicted

on TV. So she is quite used to going her own way. She knows the flickering lights are a direct communication from her missing child.

She says, "I know what I saw and I'm not crazy." And she knows what she needs: "I need you to believe me," she says to the sheriff, who is also an old friend. Unkempt, armed with an ax, with Christmas lights strung all around the house (she has put them up to facilitate further communication with Will), she certainly starts to look crazy. But, as in *Gaslight*, evidence mounts up (a photograph captures the image of a monster, a birthmark is missing from her son's supposed corpse, a stick figure drawing said to be Will's cannot be his because he draws well, like an artist), the doubters come around, and Joyce is reentered into a shared world of sorts.

We learn from Joyce Byers's example, as from Paula's, the importance of fixing on what we know and working from there in concert with others to resensitize senses deadened by domination or disaster and to find in the material world points of orientation that can be relied upon for reorientation during and after disaster. Of the two, however, Joyce is the better detective. Unlike Paula, Joyce has no treasure in the attic, no maids, no art, no breathtaking beauty; just a son, dearly loved and hidden in a clubhouse she cannot get to. Unlike Paula, Joyce does not rely on a lawman to figure out the meaning of the changing lights. Joyce, who is older than Paula and has been through more—divorced, single working mother, poor, with two kids—figures things out for herself, and though everyone starts to think she is mad, she doggedly finds a way to bring the lawman around.

By the end of *Gaslight*, Paula is single, too, but wealthy, privileged, and secure. Importantly, Paula's liberation from Gregory is not tethered to the promise of a happy marriage to another, notwithstanding a nosy neighbor's assumption to the contrary when she sees Paula and Cameron chatting on the rooftop as the film closes. The film's near-refusal of the conventional romantic happy ending is what makes it possible to see the film as a critique of (the law of) marriage, as such, and not just of this one man and this one marriage. By contrast with Cinderella, who puts on the slipper brought by the prince, Paula is not expected to try on the glove brought by Cameron; it isn't hers. Thus, the film implies that Paula will be liberated not just from Gregory but from marriage, as such, and all its fairytale promises.

It matters, surely, that Paula's rescue is not yet another episode of the traffic in women. But this mattering cuts two ways, because Paula's freedom is also not an achievement of true sex-gender equality. It seems to depend on the demasculinization of the men in her vicinity. Gregory is feminized or queered in the attic, and even Cameron himself is infantilized when he confides that the glove he brings to Paula as a kind of security was gifted to him when he was a mere boy of twelve. Paula's aunt, Alice Alquist, had joked that she had a "secret admirer" to whom she had given that missing glove, but she had never mentioned he was just a boy. When Cameron now shares that fact with Paula, she begins to trust him. Why? Is it the glove he produces as evidence, from his boyhood? Or might it be the boyhood to which he is relegated by the glove? If the latter, then female freedom means male emasculation, and that is surely a message for the film's heteronormative male viewers about what is at stake in maintaining epistemic control of their households.

This is how things play out for Jane Eyre, too, in the novel named for her. Like Paula in *Gaslight*, Jane is lied to and betrayed by the man she loves. Her employer, Mr. Rochester, lies to Jane about noises coming from the attic, and, on the day of their planned wedding, Jane finds out that Rochester is already married. (In *Gaslight*, Gregory Anton is already married, too; his wife is in Prague, Cameron tells Paula.) Rochester's first wife is Bertha Mason, a "Creole" woman he married in Jamaica, and whom he has hidden away in the attic of his English estate.[24] She was hidden away because she was mad, it is said, though we may wonder whether she has been made mad because she is locked away. Shocked by these revelations, announced by Bertha's brother who arrives in the nick of time, Jane leaves hastily, with no particular plan or destination. She is later taken in by a family named Rivers.[25] In their company, her sensibilities and self-worth regenerate. It is as if Jane knows Hannah Arendt's claim is true, that the senses rely for their sensory apprehensions not just on stimuli—which on their own can produce only irritations—but on common sense and a common world.

For women in patriarchy, though, the usual common sense is not enough, because it is not innocent. It is a gendered and raced partition of the sensible or the sensory. In such a context, where their perspectives and perceptions are devalued, some women stay true to their senses, but that is hard to sustain as individuals. Some are fortunate to

find alternative community and make kinships whose perspective rivals the dominant one. For Jane Eyre, this is the
gift of the Rivers household into which she lands. It
becomes a female household after she refuses marriage to
the brother, St. John, a missionary who departs for what
Gayatri Spivak calls his "soul-making" work abroad, in
India, only to die there.[26]

Similarly, in Toni Morrison's gothic *Home*, a vibrant
women's community serves as a place of rescue and healing.
Home rewrites the gothic/gaslight script: the gaslighting and
torture that almost kill a young woman are raced and classed,
as well as gendered. Cee, a young Black woman from a tiny
rural town, could not have less in common with *Gaslight*'s
Paula, white, wealthy, and worldly. And yet, like Paula, Cee
is haunted by childhood trauma—both stumbled, as children, onto a murdered body—orphaned, and landed in the
household of a man who seeks to take everything from her.

In Cee's case, the household belongs to Dr. Beau, a white
doctor outside Atlanta, who employs Cee, a young Black
woman, to work as his live-in helper. Unbeknownst to Cee,
the doctor likes to experiment on people. His wife tells Cee
he is "no Dr. Frankenstein," but that turns out to be true
only in the sense that Frankenstein gives birth to something,
albeit monstrous, while this doctor, who studies wombs,
monstrously kills or sickens everything he touches.[27] His
name is short for Beauregard, and he is, as his name suggests, a eugenicist.

Cee thinks she has landed in heaven. She is well-paid,
well-fed by the household's friendly Black housekeeper,
ensconced in a well-enough-appointed room, and enlisted
respectfully enough by her employer to help with his
patients. But the doctor is a Mengele who experiments on
her, and, "improving the speculum," he plumbs the depths
of her womb, nearly kills her, and leaves her barren.[28]

Like Paula, Cee *tries* early on to focus her senses on details that might help her keep her bearings. But in spite of her name, she cannot *see* what is before her eyes. For example, Cee notices the titles on the bookcases of the doctor's study: "*Out of the Night.* Must be a mystery, she thought." There *is* a mystery here but not quite in the way she thinks. The other books that catch her eye are "*The Passing of the Great Race,* and next to it, *Heredity, Race and Society.*" She resolves to study and understand what the educated man reads: "How small, how useless was her schooling, she thought, and promised herself she would find time to read about and understand 'eugenics.'"[29]

In the end she will be schooled, but not by those books. After she is rescued, a superior sensory education is freely provided her by a group of illiterate Black women who had "the skills of the illiterate: perfect memory, photographic minds, keen sense of smell and hearing."[30] Cee is brought, nearly dead, by her brother Frank to the women healers back in their hometown of Lotus, Georgia. The women banish Frank from their midst. "They believed his maleness would worsen her condition."[31] And they return Cee to full sensation, drawing on quirky practices of restoration. She is instructed to lie with her legs open to the sun for an hour every day. "Sun-smacked" is their cure for the shell-shocked. When Cee says, "How could I have known what he was up to?," these "country women who loved mean" reply, "Misery don't call ahead. That's why you have to stay awake—otherwise it just walks in your door." And Cee comes to understand: "She had been stupid, eager to please." She learns from Miss Ethel, who says, "Look to yourself, You free. Nothing and nobody is obliged to save you but you. Seed your own land." It is a lesson we cannot be sure Paula learns, but Cee does: "She wanted to be the one who rescued her own self."[32]

These women, women with their "seen-it-all-eyes," see what Cee could not. They are schooled in the shock politics of whiteness. They know they could lose their little bit of land to white violence any time any day, but they nonetheless invest in their garden. They build a buffer of faith, without illusions about its fragility. The buffer is made of the world's tatters, woven together in the garden that beautifies land into vital ground, and they turn rags into folk quilts that tourists buy for money. In this setting, Cee is repatterned back into herself: "She could know the truth, accept it, and keep on quilting."[33] But she is not whole.

In Morrison's *Home* and in *Jane Eyre* and *Gaslight*, the women's freedom and power seem to depend on the demasculinization or de-eroticization of the men in their vicinity or on their banishment. With St. John gone, Jane lives for a time with the Rivers sisters in a women's-only household. When she returns to Rochester, he has been hobbled and blinded. The cause was a fire at his home that also killed Bertha Mason, who found a way finally to assert her truth against her husband's deceit. Jane will marry Rochester, but he is now dependent on her care, which means the partnership is more maternal than marital. In some sense, then, might he have remained married to Bertha Mason, after all? In another female gothic, Daphne du Maurier's *Rebecca*, the story ends with the new Mrs. de Winter displacing her troubled matrimonial relation to her husband with a new maternal one. "I held my arms out to him and he came to me like a child."[34] So, too, in *Gaslight*, Cameron is infantilized, subtly, when he presents himself to Paula as the twelve-year-old he once was. And in *Home*, Cee, who is told she cannot bear children, enters into a non-erotic domestic partnership with her brother, Frank, for whom she cooks and homekeeps. Is the freedom achieved by gothic women only the small freedom that comes from being moved off the register of erotic heterosexuality and onto a maternal plane?[35] Is that a freedom at all?

Feminist criticism might seem a small freedom, too; its careful reading more a balm, or placebo, than a canny tactic for those caught in a storm of patriarchal inequality or trapped inside on its sunny days. Feminist criticism is powerful because it devotes itself to detail in order to ground itself, and, by chasing wild threads of meaning, it recreates the fabric of what Arendt called the in-between on which worldliness depends.[36] It does its forensic and fabulist work compassed by the sensory and the normative, attentive to their coimplication in the partition of the sensible that is patriarchy and its partners.

3

The President's House Is Empty

Inauguration Day

A detail stood out when, after the November 2016 presidential election but before his inauguration, Donald Trump announced that his family would not live in the White House. His wife, Melania, and son Barron preferred to live in New York, he said. At the time, no one objected. The assumption seemed to be that this was simply a matter of personal choice for which the country would bear the costs. But "personal choice" is part of an ideology of neoliberalism that includes patriarchy and is elastic enough to cover even for this unconventional arrangement of twin households and wifely independence.

Melania and Barron ultimately moved to the White House on June 12, 2017, but the costs of the Trump family's two households were billed to the public. The additional security necessitated by the decision to maintain a second household in New York City is expensive. Security alone is estimated to be about $24 million.[1] And there were other costs, too: repeated presidential flights to New York, motorcades in and out of midtown Manhattan and, throughout

Trump's term, to Florida airports and Palm Springs. In office, Trump made numerous trips to golf on his own courses, at a cost of about $3 million per trip. Many of them have been to his Florida resort, Mar-a-Lago, which he likes to call his "winter White House," while nonetheless billing his security detail as much as 650 dollars a night for each of the rooms they are obliged to stay in to protect him.[2]

From the start, many of those costs, racked up on Trump properties, were paid right into the president's own pockets. For example, according to the *New York Post*, in addition to "the cost of agents, staff and equipment and barriers that are normal in such cases," security services protecting Trump's family in New York were obliged to *rent space* in Trump Tower at a cost of more than $3 million a year, to be paid to the president's own corporation.[3] Secret Service agents protecting Trump in Florida and also in New Jersey were billed—we, the public, were billed—for their use of golf carts to follow him on his rounds. Although *Politico* reported that Trump footed the bill for Japanese prime minister Shinzō Abe's stay at Mar-a-Lago (waived the bill might be more accurate), it was also reported that Trump promised to donate all money spent by foreign governments at his hotels to the Treasury so that he would not violate the Constitution's Emoluments Clause. But there is no sign such donations have been made. On May 16, 2017, congressional Democrats introduced legislation that would order Trump to reimburse the federal government for any public money spent on trips to his private resorts. The bill went nowhere, and the bipartisan congressional budget of that same month guaranteed the federal government would pay New York for costs incurred protecting Melania's Trump Tower household.

This is galling, because we already pay for a secure home and office for the president of the United States and his family. It is called the White House. The White House is a public thing to be used by the president and his or her family while in public office. The White House has an infrastructure of security that provides presidents and their families with the protection they need. Trump and his family opted out of that public thing. They chose to go private. And in so doing, they incurred costs that they then passed on to the public. Their "free choice" was subsidized by the public, as are so many of the supposedly "free" choices exercised by others (charter schools, gated neighborhoods, Humvees, private airplanes).

The public thing, the White House, enables certain efficiencies in the provision of security and administrative support, but these are lost when the private option is preferred. A president, or his family, who lives at private home(s) requires a mobile security apparatus and governance infrastructure that the White House does not. The American public even provides the president with a holiday home, Camp David, which, because of its long use by past presidents, also has in place the necessary infrastructure. However, Trump has spurned this home as well: "Have you seen it?" he said of Camp David, as if to explain his preference for his own commercial golf resort, Mar-a-Lago. Is it not obvious that if a president disdains the homes the public provides for him, and thus forgoes their efficiencies, the resulting costs should be borne by him (he is the one who has opted out) and not by the very public whose public thing he has spurned? Trump's family may be free to not use the residence provided by the public, but they should be personally responsible for assuming the costs of that choice rather than passing them on to us. Attending to this neglected detail highlights the extent to which mainstream American political media have absorbed neoliberal assumptions and are no longer critical of them.

Beyond the monetary costs of the Trump opt-out, there are symbolic costs, as well. Here there may even be a lesson for Trump. Faced with the refusal of Mexico to pay for the much-promised border wall, Trump has said he expects U.S. taxpayers to pay for it (promising vaguely that Mexico will pay us back). But taxpayers have lost the habit of happily paying for public things, and Trump, the one opting out, is in no position to revivify the habit. After years of neoliberalization, the reservoir of love for public things in the U.S. is diminished.[4] Neoliberalism means many things to many people, but the one trait by which it is always distinguished is its approval of the opt-out and a willingness to turn a blind eye to its hidden costs.

Everything is optional for the neoliberal; this is how neoliberalism defines freedom. Neoliberals opt out of any collective thing they can afford to opt out of. They believe everyone should be free to send their children to private or charter schools, to live in private gated communities, to hire private transport rather than take the school bus, to walk around without a mask in a pandemic. "Choice" is their watchword, and choice is synonymous with freedom.

The hidden costs of opting out are not their problem, neoliberals say. But they are ours. If the well-to-do do not use the public school system, the community is deprived of their energies and contributions. If they do not use city roads and sewage, the well-to-do come to resent having to pay for the upkeep of infrastructure. If fewer and fewer children take the school bus, it soon becomes an added expense to the public purse that cannot be justified, and suddenly there is no bus service, even if some need it; or else it costs extra, and only its users are asked to pay for it, which raises costs for some and singles some people out in a supposedly "public" system. And, of course, those who refuse to wear masks endanger everyone. These issues ran through debates about repealing the Affordable Care Act as well, early in 2017. Some congressmen asked why the healthy should "subsidize" the sick, thus betraying little understanding of the workings of insurance (in which those who are healthy now pay to indemnify them*selves* against the contingency of one day becoming sick) and of the very idea of democracy (in which redistributions are made to underwrite social equilibria that benefit everyone and public health is a public good that all of us enjoy together, just as we all suffer—though not necessarily equally, since we are not equally vulnerable or exposed—when there is a public pandemic).

But there is a still worse cost here—to democracy as such. The democratic experiment involves living cheek by jowl with others, sharing classrooms, roads, and buses, paying for them together, complaining about them together, and sometimes even praising and enjoying them together, as picnickers will do on a sunny afternoon in Central Park. One of the many sad ironies here is that Central Park—landscape architecture's ode to the power of democratic beauty—is just a stone's throw away from where barricades encircled Trump Tower from January to June 2017 to protect Melania. That a meme began, calling to "free Melania," shows just how absorptive neoliberal culture is, capable of turning a precious gothic detail that highlights a world of misogynist injustice into a pet theme freed of the original's powers of perception and prescription. She does not need freeing.

Opting out usually depends on the public purse it pretends to circumvent. Charter schools and voucher programs invite locals to opt out of public schools while drawing on public funds that might have improved the public education system rather than provide an alternative to it. Someone is making money on charter schools and vouchers, and it is not the community. Also, and more importantly—as Senator Maggie Hassan pointed out to Betsy DeVos at her

confirmation hearing to become secretary of education—
charter schools and voucher programs are not governed by
public education's democratic mandate to educate *all* stu-
dents. Like the Affordable Care Act, which mandates providing health care coverage to those with preexisting conditions,
a properly democratic education system mandates providing
education to those with preexisting conditions, too, such as
poverty, recent immigration, and physical and learning dis-
abilities, as well as other challenges that may make learning
difficult or require special attention. This democratic mandate to educate everyone is what charters and voucher systems opt out of. Such mandates are the last, dying breath of
the public thing.

The latest and most public opt-outs under this presidency—wear a mask or don't, it is your choice!—show just
how costly opt-outs are. They derail collective action and
destroy the public thing, as is evidenced by the Trump First
Family's cavalier attitude toward the White House, a reminder
of the emptiness of this presidency that cannot be obscured,
not even by full-body huggings of the flag.

4
He Said, He Said
The Feminization of James Comey

After he was fired by Trump, the now former head of the FBI James Comey was so rapidly feminized you would think he was J. Edgar Hoover. In June 2017 Laura Ingraham claimed that Comey is a "drama queen" who writes in an unmanly way. Charles Payne said Comey is "a lot more emotional than you would think the head of the FBI should be . . . and vindictive too." Amy Holmes said the fired FBI director is "like a thirteen-year-old girl," while a CNN commentator offered that Comey couldn't "cowboy up, couldn't man up." Then there is this from the president's son Donald Trump Jr.: "So if he was a 'Stronger guy' he might have actually followed procedure & the law? You were the director of the FBI, who are you kidding?"[1] This is not just a story of the once-mighty brought low, but of the particular techniques of feminization by which Donald Trump and his allies force people's compliance or secure their destruction.

That Trump seeks to diminish or humiliate those around him is no secret. That such abjection often takes the form of feminization is also widely known. But how to counter it all?

Recall Chris Christie's account of a dinner with Trump and some others; Trump says, "There's the menu, you guys order whatever you want," then he says, "Chris, you and I are going to have the meatloaf." Why didn't Christie refuse to play the role of wife in Trump's 1950s supper-club fantasy? He could have said no, I'll have the steak. But he didn't.

We do not know if Trump ordered for Comey at their now famous dinner in January 2017. But we do know that something similar occurred. Trump let the FBI director know that he had certain expectations of this man who served at his pleasure, and Comey, at least according to his critics in the media and in the Senate, did not protest enough. (Later, two years later, some of the same people will protest that Adam Schiff did not work hard enough to make the case for impeachment in the House before bringing it to the Senate, making it his fault that they voted against impeachment.)

During the Senate Intelligence Committee's hearing, Comey's feminization was apparent to women watching it. In a *New York Times* op-ed, Nicole Serratore said that it was like watching the interrogation of a woman who has accused a man of sexual harassment.[2] In fact, several of the questions, posed to Comey, were almost identical to those asked of Anita Hill at another famous Senate hearing about how best to respond to a boss's improper overtures. Why did you keep coming into work even after you say he made you feel uncomfortable? Why did you take no action at the time? Are you sure he really meant that? You said you didn't want to be left alone with him again but then you took his phone calls. In the words of Republican Senator Blunt, "So. . . . why didn't you say, 'I'm not taking that call. You need to talk to the Attorney General'?" Senator Feinstein also expressed surprise at Comey's failure to live up to the demands of masculinity: "You're big, you're strong," she said, "why didn't you stop and say, 'Mr. President, this is wrong—I cannot discuss that with you'?"

In all these questions, one key question is repeated: Why should we believe *you*?

The problem for Comey is that power consists in that question never being asked. Believability is a structural privilege that comes with straight white manhood. Its loss is an effect of feminization. So—what to do? How to respond? To answer is weakness. To not answer is weakness. He tried obliqueness. His mother did not raise him to crow about himself, he said, meaning thereby to certify his own good character. But, by invoking his mother, Comey risked the inference of "mommy's boy." This is weak tea as far as fending off feminization is concerned. And, once feminized, a man's efforts to defend himself may start to sound, well, defensive; his insistence on his integrity is easily cast as self-absorption; and his reliance on the testimony of old friends can seem needy. Gender has a slippery way of recoding everything. Before you know it, the authority that let you publicly chide Hillary Clinton for email carelessness is gone. Suddenly you have gone from being head of one of the most powerful security apparatuses in the world to being a *showboat*, as Trump said of Comey, using a 1950s supper-club word. It can happen to anyone. Just ask Sean Spicer, Jeff Sessions, or John Kelly.

Independence has been Comey's accustomed position, granted him by institutional and sex-gender affiliations: head of the FBI and a straight white male in America. But, like so many men, he assumed his worth and independence were his because of his character, signs of his personal fortitude. So it is not surprising that Comey himself falls into the trap of describing what happened at that fateful January dinner as the result of his lacking, perhaps, a certain strength.

When Trump said, "I need loyalty, I expect loyalty," Comey did not yield, but neither did he overtly protest. As he said in his statement, "I didn't move, speak, or change my facial expression in any way during the awkward silence that followed. We simply looked at each other in silence." Comey will later say that "maybe if I were stronger," he would have done more. But silence ought to have been enough. Silence is usually associated in American political culture with masculinity, as in the phrase "the strong, silent type." That strength is obscured, though, even from Comey himself, and with Diane Feinstein's help, by his feminization. It is in the context of his feminization, then, that we should hear Comey's reflection at the Senate hearing that perhaps he should have spoken up. For women, after all, silence means not strength but consent or submission (or so we are told daily by the men who pay women for their silence, via non-disclosure agreements).

If we think of gender not as a personal trait but as an apparatus of power, we can better understand the key role it played in Comey's confusion at that dinner with Trump. Comey was confused because, as he reports, Trump asked Comey that night whether he wanted the job that Trump had already, twice earlier, told him was his. But Comey was also confused because Trump "invited me to dinner that night, saying he was going to invite my whole family, but decided to have just me this time, with the whole family coming the next time. It was unclear from the conversation who else would be at the dinner, although I assumed there would be others." There would be no others, because the aim that night was to get Comey to be submissive. There was a carrot: his family might get invited to some future dinner at the White House! And there was a stick: did he want the job that was but wasn't his? Trump did not get the submission he wanted, and so the aim ever since has been to demolish

Comey. Recast as a "thirteen-year-old girl," the former FBI director's credibility is suddenly in question. He seems trapped in an alien maze of "he said, he said."

This is surely why, at one point in his testimony, Comey found reason to mention his wife. This detail did not receive the attention it deserves. *Business Insider* went for the punchline but missed the joke, reporting that "in a rare moment of levity during former FBI Director James Comey's testimony before the Senate Intelligence Committee on Thursday, Comey said that he wished he had skipped a private dinner with President Donald Trump in order to keep a date with his wife."[3] Why was it funny? Imagine skipping dinner with the president to keep a date with . . . your wife? Isn't it obviously laughable? Except there is more to it: the bad joke allowed Comey to bring up his wife, and this he did as a way to reestablish the gender privilege he once took for granted. Having a wife, being a straight white man with a wife and children (six, no less), is still the most secure sign of credibility in American politics. No wonder Comey reached for it. But it did not work, not this time. It turns out gender really is constructed. And no one understands that better than those who most loudly reject that insight: self-proclaimed conservative supporters of Trump and the great feminizer-in-chief himself, all of them deeply invested in gender as an apparatus of power—as long as they are in charge of it.

Just a year later, we saw the apparatus of gender at work again, after the Helsinki summit between Trump and Putin. But this time it was the great feminizer-in-chief who was feminized: the popular press depicted Trump as subservient to his Russian master, a "pushover," as retiring senator Jeff Flake put it.[4] Feminist critics could relish this new development. But feminization boomerangs, and in the end resorting to it will only reinforce, not undo, the misogyny we live with every day. Although Trump's feminization may satisfy critics in the short term, it also sets the stage for what will surely follow: a call to return things to "normal" by electing a real man in his place, one day. Let's not join that old chorus.[5]

Besides, those of us who follow the gender politics of power know how malleable feminization is. Notably, Trump is one of the few who can make it work *for* him. If he almost never resorts to naming his wife, that is because stabilizing his gender is not his aim. His act, at his rallies, is a blend of male domination and female victimization. One minute, he promises to dominate others; the next, he complains of persecution. His voice alters from a guttural rumble that threatens ("Get him outta here!") to a soprano that wheedles and lilts ("So I said to them, slow the testing down, please"). As we shall see in later essays in this volume, he is the voice of both Lisa Page and Peter Strzok when he simulates passionate scenes between them. When he mocks other women, he impersonates them with a voice so feminized that most American men could not risk it when speaking in public. This habitual ambi-gendering was made clear toward the end of Trump's (first?) term when, sick with Covid-19, he was to be released from the hospital and considered appearing before his supporters in a dress shirt that he would rip off to reveal a Superman T-shirt underneath. "They'd love it!" he certainly imagined. In the end, he opted instead to rip off his face mask while standing atop a White House a balcony, and, just a few short days later, he channeled Evita from the same high perch for a short mini-rally of (some paid) supporters.

Such ambi-gendering is a source of Trump's rhetorical and political power. It sets him up for his followers as both their defender and in need of their defending while inoculating him against the worst of feminization. It does nothing to destabilize the often punitive heteronormative sex-gender binary. The norm that others, like Comey, are punished for violating seems to be Trump's for the taking. But if gender has a way of recoding everything, then it may yet be that Trump himself will one day find himself on the wrong side of its apparatus.

5

The Members-Only President Goes to Alabama

Police officers are required to guard the heads of people they arrest as they load them into the back seat of a police car, lest they bump their heads. It is made necessary by the handcuffs, which put people off balance. At a gathering of police in the summer of 2017, Trump told them they should reconsider the gesture. "Please don't be too nice," he said, as if niceness was the issue: "You can take the hand away, okay?" The police officers lined up behind him all laughed as if to say: okay. Really at issue was not any supposed niceness, but the fact that an officer's hand on a suspect's head is an iconic instance of public care, increasingly rare in our nearly post-welfare state democracy.

The requirement of public care is often, even routinely, ignored or violated, as the name Freddie Gray so painfully reminds us. Arrested in Baltimore in April 2015, Gray was beaten, "shackled by his hands and feet," tossed into a police van, "but unrestrained by a seatbelt," and taken on a "rough ride" by police. The van's sharp turns and quick accelerations and decelerations bounced him around in the back.

He "couldn't protect himself from the impact as he crashed into the interior of the vehicle," and he suffered a fatal spinal cord injury. He died a week later.[1]

Gray was not seated in the back seat of a cruiser with a hand hovering over his head, though he had every right to that gesture and the care it represents. That outstretched hand, owed to any- and everyone, including the criminal, the indigent, the suspect, the marginal, the unfortunate, the needy, is especially voluble these days. Perhaps that is why the president singled it out for his disapproval.

And the police heard. They had been dishing out violence to minorities already, but now they were further emboldened. Three and a half years into Trump's term, in Minneapolis, in 2020, the police killed George Floyd, an unarmed, Black U.S. citizen, in the street. A brave seventeen-year-old filmed it, and the world was then able to watch as the life was slowly pressed out of this man by a police officer casually pressing his knee to Floyd's neck. The insouciance of the officer's gaze into the camera as it recorded his illegal murderous act was remarkable. Two other officers knelt on Floyd's back, too, and, though he complained repeatedly he could not breathe, no officer let up for almost nine minutes. By then, he was dead. Minneapolis Police Union president Bob Kroll, an ardent Trump supporter, defended the police action. In a letter to police union members, Kroll, with no evidence, described Floyd as a "violent criminal," and, again with no evidence, he called those protesting Floyd's death "terrorists."[2] His clear message was that neither Floyd nor those who protested his killing had a right to public care. That is false, though: in fact, even criminals and terrorists do have that right. And it is important to hold on to that right because the hovering hand dismissed by Trump is the counter of the knee to the neck: one of the few signs we have in public life of the dignity of persons, as such.

Two and a half years earlier, the 2017 Unite the Right rally in Charlottesville, Virginia, exemplified a different kind of public care. The Alt Right and neo-Nazis who marched that day understood the importance of caring and being cared for in public. One man poured milk over another's face to counter the effects of Mace, then gently tilted his fellow Nazi's chin in his hand as if to ask: was that better? One of the things that drew the Alt-Right marchers to gather was the desire to practice such care in public. The march's organizers noted the importance of coming out, being seen, working together in real life. "We don't have the camaraderie," one Alt-Right marcher said, "we don't have the trust level that our rivals do . . . and that camaraderie and trust is built up through activism." Describing themselves as "showing up," being "part of a larger whole," and "having a great time," the marchers made clear their desire to create the conditions for mutual care rather than private isolation. Through the public performance of camaraderie, they were building trust, care, and concern. They wanted to generate power. But they succeeded mostly in unleashing violence. Heather Heyer was murdered that day and many others injured when a Unite the Right rally-goer drove his car at breakneck speed into a crowd of counter-protesters.[3]

The public the Alt Right want to be part of is a fantasy, exclusively white, and so the busy, messy, conflicted space of public life and activism now does not answer to their desire, though it does offer what they crave. Public life is full of care for others and, as Hannah Arendt would put it, care for a world we share with others. But to belong to that world, you have to be willing to take your place among plural others who are different from you. And this, the Alt-Right marchers were not willing to do. Chanting "Jews will not replace us," the men at that march in Charlottesville wanted the world without the share. They wanted a public, but just for themselves. This is the dangerous dream of all ethno-nationalists and white supremacists: *they want the public, without the politics.*

The Alt-Right demand for public life is part of a quest to retake the public they or their parents abandoned a few decades ago when public things were integrated in the U.S. After desegregation, white disinvestment and abandonment of public things often come next. One example, explored by Jeff Wiltse, in *Contested Waters: A Social History of Swimming Pools in America,* is public swimming pools, which were racially desegregated in the late 1940s and 1950s and then abandoned by whites. "In city after city after city . . . the overall attendance to the pool would plummet," Wiltse says. Whites "didn't stop swimming. . . . They built private club pools, which [could] legally discriminate against black Americans. Or they built at-home residential pools, so they could really enclose themselves off from the larger public and truly exercise control over who they were swimming with."[4]

Trump's preference for his private, members-only club Mar-a-Lago over the White House is also a preference for the private pool over the public thing. What Mar-a-Lago members buy with their $200,000 membership fee (doubled after Trump was elected president) is control over access and the company they keep. Here neoliberalism, which promotes privatization for its own reasons, aligns with white supremacy, which seeks above all to restrict membership and control access in a diverse democracy. When, in June 2020, Trump had a wall built around the White House during the D.C. protests of George Floyd's killing, he showed again his predilection for the private over the public thing.

Decades after abandoning public life rather than see it integrated, emboldened by a president and a party that coddle rather than condemn them, white supremacists want to experience public enjoyment but without the divisions and conflicts, thrills and risks, wins and losses that vivify contemporary public life. Perhaps the same is true of police in St. Louis, Missouri, who, in September 2017, having cleared a street of protestors, went on to take also the protestors' chant—"Whose streets? Our streets!"—as if that chant, and the hard-earned civic power that gave rise to it, and the public roadways themselves were the police's for the taking. But the protestors are part of the very public the police are meant to serve. In the wake of the bench trial acquittal of former St. Louis patrolman Jason Stockley for the 2011 killing of Anthony Lamar Smith, protestors' calls for justice and racial equality are worthy of care and concern, not mockery and theft.

The office of the U.S. presidency has an obligation to model care and express concern for the nation, without feminizing the public into dependence. The public, after all, is the president's boss. He reports to us. But the current president's care is uncaring, and his voice loudly telegraphs a lack of concern. At a rally in Alabama in October 2017, just a few weeks after the Unite the Right March attacked Charlottesville, Trump spoke of his Twitter tiffs with Kim Jong Un and described vividly the dangers that could be unleashed. North Korea could explode a "massive weapon," Trump said, and that could cause "tremendous, tremendous calamity where the plume goes." Perhaps sensing some anxiety in the crowd, Trump then told the crowd not to worry. "Maybe something gets worked out and maybe it doesn't, but I can tell you one thing: You are protected. Okay? You are protected. Nobody's going to mess with our people." And later: "You'll be okay. We won't let anything happen to you."

This expression of care dangerously and disingenuously positioned the crowd as personally dependent on him and his personal kindness—"we won't let anything happen to you"—rather than bound together, by his office, to each other and to others, too, as citizens of a diverse, powerful, and potentially vulnerable electorate. Moreover, Trump used this paternalistic care to draw an exceptional circle around white Alabamians, to whom he improbably dared to claim he belonged. "I understand the people of Alabama. I feel like I'm from Alabama, frankly," the president said. "Isn't it a little weird when a guy who lives on Fifth Avenue in the most beautiful apartment you've ever seen, comes to Alabama and Alabama loves that guy? I mean, it's crazy. It's crazy." It is.

He closed the circle of belonging that bound him to his Alabama audience, most of whom could never gain access to his Manhattan apartment, much less Mar-a-Lago, by referring to Black athletes of conscience like Colin Kaeper-nick as "sons of bitches" and calling for team owners to throw off the field any athletes who kneel in protest during the national anthem. Individual athletes as well as coaches and teams responded for a time by drawing their own circles of belonging, taking the knee en masse, linking arms in solidarity, and the NFL rebuffed his instruction to fire pro-testing players (though not one of the league's teams to this day has managed to hire Kaepernick, even though in 2020 the protests are now normalized).

But, in Alabama, the people at the rally know what they heard. The president has their backs. And they know that, in the unlikely event any of them is ever arrested, they will not get a "rough ride" or a knee to the neck. They know that they will be put in the back seat of a police car, with some-one's hand surely hovering carefully over their heads and they will arrive at the police station alive and with their spinal cord intact.[5]

6

An Empire unto Himself?

Harvey Weinstein's Downfall

"We're an empire now," Karl Rove reportedly said to Ron Suskind in 2004, "and when we act, we create our own reality." These words now reverberate, well over a decade later, in the wake of the Harvey Weinstein scandal.

Sexual abuse is about power over the victim, but, for men like Weinstein, it is also about control over reality. The latter is the kind of power that was in play for Weinstein when he violated so many women over many years. For Weinstein, the sex—a rote pattern of predatory behavior, endlessly rehearsed and reperformed like his own personal Groundhog Day—was a move in a longer game that begins with the trap (a business meeting in a hotel room, perhaps with a female assistant present as "honeypot") and ends with the cover-up that is surely the most enduring excitement: the sheer pleasure of power over reality itself.

The very vernacular of the crime emphasizes what is at stake: "Do you really want to make an enemy for five minutes of your time?" Five minutes? "It steals something," is all Hope Exiner D'Amore can bring herself to say about her experience with Weinstein in the 1970s when he was still a concert promoter.[1] Later, as a famous film producer, he would say, *You can be a star in my world or you can be nobody.* Or, *No one will believe you.* Most women know the fear of being disbelieved. Almost no women know the power of saying, "No one will believe you."

Such threats and promises advertise a man's control over reality, the pleasure of which is enhanced, apparently, if someone else (your victim, your assistants, fellow executives, or an entire company) is watching while you do it. Maybe that is why Rove shared his little secret, that day in 2004, with Suskind. It is certainly why Donald Trump bragged about his pussy-grabbing secrets to Billy Bush on what became known as the *Access Hollywood* tape, the name eerily signaling not just the name of the show Billy Bush hosted, but the braggadocio of Trump who, to hear him tell it, had *access to all of Hollywood:* "When you're a star, they let you do it." That proclaimed permission is belied, however, by the signed nondisclosure agreements (NDAs) and the catch and kill deals of the *National Inquirer.* Turns out "they" don't just "let" you; you actually have to purchase their silence, or trick them, or bully and threaten them into not telling and discredit them if they do.

Trump and Weinstein differ in one crucial way, however. Weinstein is old-school. He feared exposure. He tried to negotiate with his accusers and those who believed them. In his first responses to the charges leveled against him, he denied the sex was nonconsensual but conceded there might be differences of opinion or perspective. He emailed friends asking for support. He promised to seek treatment and asked for another chance. These used to be moves in the reality-control game. But in the age of Rove and Trump, trading accusations with your accusers, conceding anything to them, means you are already, in Trump's grade school terms, a loser: reality's victim, not its maker.

It was an act of reality-domination of Rovian proportions to do what Trump did before the second presidential debate during the 2016 election season. Rather than distance himself from the scandal aired just days earlier by the *Access Hollywood* tape, Trump greedily embraced it, creating a reality in which he, without a hint of shame, took on the role of defender of women wronged. As more credible reports of women charging him with assault surfaced, Trump gathered around him three women who claimed to have been sexually assaulted by the husband of his opponent. And he asked them to speak about their experience. It surely never occurred to Hillary Clinton, Trump's Democratic opponent in the 2016 election, to surround herself with the victims of Trump's predations. Think of it: they could have been by her side, women like Stormy Daniels (who had not yet signed her election-eve nondisclosure agreement, though she had been threatened to stay silent), Karen McDougall, and all the others. They would not have had to speak. They could have just sat there, perhaps with tape over their mouths marked with the letters N.D.A.

But Clinton was still playing by the old rules, and so was the press. The lag between the old rules and the new ones played in Trump's favor. His lack of shame was taken by some to show not a new horrifying kind of shamelessness, but rather innocence of the charges, or at the very least, evidence of their irrelevance. Everybody does it!

Obama was playing by the old rules, too, when he warned of Trump, "Reality has a way of catching up with you." (The impact of Covid-19 on the American population and, later, on Trump himself may yet prove the forty-fourth president prophetic.) On the other side is Trump, who believes reality itself can be dominated. Not shaped, or sold, or denied, not even made, in the Madison Avenue style of *Mad Men*. Dominated. In this sense, notwithstanding the protestations of many never-Trump neoconservatives until now, Trump is a creature of Rove's Republicanism: an empire unto himself.

Weinstein, by contrast, lost control of the newspapers he thought were in his grasp. And he was tried, found guilty, and sentenced to prison for some of his crimes. Once upon a time, the verdict in the Weinstein case, and the sentence, might have been a happy ending. The moral of the story would have been that violence against women calls for justice, journalism exposes abuses of power, and law can call powerful men to account. It is a good story. Its headline might be, "Patriarchy dies in the disinfecting light of day." Indeed, one reason so many followed the Weinstein story is that his arrest seemed to promise a world in which actions have consequences, truth has power, and good people fight to further it, and sometimes they win. Imagine that.

But now the news of Weinstein's sentencing is one good day in a larger struggle to recover what we have almost lost: a world in which journalism has an impact and the infrastructures that support it are sturdy and effective. These include a really free, well-funded, and diverse press, more reporters who worry less about access than about corruption and the abuse of power, a public with the capacity to be shocked, voters willing and able to exercise the power of the ballot, ungerrymandered districts with the power to affect electoral outcomes, paper trails for voting rather than reliance on untrustworthy voting machines, a legislative branch willing to do its job, and the real possibility that a once-powerful man can be brought down by the truth.

7

Race and the Revolving Door of (Un)Reality TV

With a Reality TV president in office, it should be no surprise to see the revolving door between reality and TV swing around and leave us unclear about which side of it we are on. And yet I am nonetheless stunned at the usefulness of the HBO show *VEEP* in helping us understand Trump in Washington.

The central character in *VEEP* is Selina Meyer, an empty, ambitious woman who will do or say anything to get what she wants, impervious to the impact on others. In Season 6, episode 8 of the show, Selina's devoted assistant, Gary, after five-and-a-half seasons of servility, finally gets Selina to come to his hometown, meet his parents, and attend a party he is throwing.[1] Before the party, Gary shares a beloved childhood story with Selina. Later, Selina, who is trying to impress one of the guests with her folksiness, folds Gary's memory into her own toast. "The betrayal," says Jessica Goldstein, "leaves him speechless, and, as usual, Selina is cavalier about the pain her actions have caused."[2]

This, I imagine, was the scene in the Oval Office in mid-October, 2017, when General Kelly, Trump's second chief of staff, shared privately his story of his son's death, using language that military men use for such things. "He knew what he signed up for." "He understood the mission." Or, perhaps, as he put it later, he "was doing exactly what he wanted to do when he was killed. . . . He knew what he was getting into. . . . He knew what the possibilities were because we were at war." Kelly probably told the private story because he was attempting to dissuade Trump from placing calls to the families of U.S. soldiers who died in Niger on October 4, 2017. "Sir, there's nothing you can do to lighten the burden on these families," Kelly says he told Trump. Kelly also told Trump that when his own son died in Afghanistan in 2010, he never got a call from Obama. Was Kelly perhaps thinking the disclosure would free Trump to not call? It had precisely the opposite effect, kicking the president into his characteristic one-upmanship with the one man he can never stop trying to beat.

Shortly after his chat with Kelly, Trump was asked at a press conference about why he had not yet spoken about the four dead in Niger, and Trump, channeling *VEEP*'s Selina, tells part of what Kelly told him: Obama didn't call everyone, actually, he didn't call Kelly when his son died, for example, but he, Trump, will. Later, he calls the family of one of the four American men who died in Niger. But things do not go well. His words do not console; they infuriate. That is because they are not his words.

Talking to Myeshia Johnson, the widow of deceased sergeant La David Johnson, Trump uses the words and phrases he heard Kelly use. They are manly phrases, like "he knew what he signed up for!" When Kelly said those words, Trump was impressed. He probably thought if he stole the words, he would look and sound like Kelly and not like a draft-evading, cavalier, military wannabe with fake bone spurs. But not only is Trump no John Kelly. Trump is no Selina Meyer. He couldn't pull it off. He seemed not to know the name of the soldier who died. When she got off the phone, Myeshia Johnson cried, "He didn't even know his name. He kept calling him, 'Your guy.'" Worse yet, the words offered as consolation were offensive because they are the kinds of words men and women in the armed forces say to each other, maybe, but not to the bereaved. They are not the words Kelly would have said to his own wife, Karen, about their lost son when, as he says, he went upstairs to break her heart with the news of his death. And so when Trump stole the words for himself, to say them to the wrong people, at the wrong time, in the wrong way, they felt foul, *VEEP*-level foul.

Trump rejected the criticism that followed and called on Kelly, who had been on the call, to back him up. (It was only the first of several presidential calls that Trump would go on to insist were "very nice" or "perfect." See also Lt. Col. Vindman, whistleblower, Ukraine.) Kelly obliged and said the call was "a respectful expression of presidential sympathies." But Congresswoman Frederica Wilson of Florida had heard the call, too. When the call came in, she was with the Johnson family, waiting with the widow and her children on the tarmac for the plane carrying Sgt. Johnson's remains home for burial. Wilson confirmed the new widow's account of the call and said that she, too, was offended by what the president said. "'So in other words, when you sign up when you go into the military, you are really signing up to die,' she said of the president's comments. "That is not what you say to a grieving widow, a woman who just learned that her husband cannot have an open casket funeral. In fact, she will probably not even be able to see his body.'"[3]

Now Kelly was in deep. He had called the call "respectful" and "presidential," expecting no rebuttals. He accused the congresswoman of politicizing the matter and described her as "listening in" on the phone call, as if illicitly. But the call had been on speakerphone, and Wilson was not listening in but providing support to a grieving family in her community, herself in mourning, too, for a man she had known since he was in elementary school and took part in a mentoring program she started.

Soon, Sarah Huckabee Sanders and others chimed in, too; they backed up the president's claims, but this just further fed the fire. The back and forth continued until, finally, trying to put an end to the matter, Kelly moved to discredit Wilson.

He had another story about her. He had been "stunned," he said, two years earlier by public comments she made at a ceremony dedicating a new building in Florida to two FBI agents who were killed on the job. "And a congresswoman stood up, and in a long tradition of empty barrels making the most noise, stood up there in all of that and talked about how she was instrumental in getting the funding for that building, and how she took care of her constituents because she got the money, and she just called up President (Barack) Obama, and on that phone call, he gave the money, the $20 million, to build the building, and she sat down," he said. "And we were stunned, stunned that she'd done it. Even for someone that is that empty a barrel, we were stunned."[4]

It was a turn to the security blanket of whiteness, an astoundingly disrespectful and racist lie. To say that Wilson, who is Black, boasted that President Obama just handed her 20 million dollars is to slander both her and the former president. But this time there was a tape: the *Sun Sentinel* had a video of the building dedication ceremony, and it exposed as false Kelly's version of the story: Wilson "had not taken credit for the building's funding," nor had she claimed to have Obama on speed dial. She had only had a hand in the building's naming, in any case, not its funding, which was approved before she was elected. And she had fully honored the new building's namesakes at the ceremony.[5] James Comey, who also spoke that day, had singled her out for praise, though, and thanked her for her work on the project. Perhaps that is what somehow stuck in Kelly's mind. Or maybe it was his craw.

When Kelly said, falsely, that Wilson's "grandstanding" remarks focused more on her own actions than the heroism of the two FBI agents, he implied there was a pattern here and that with Sgt. Johnson she was at it again, stealing someone else's moment for her own purposes. It is always all about her, Kelly seemed to say, projecting onto Rep. Wilson qualities he had no doubt come to know intimately in Trump's Oval Office.

But now the revolving door of (un)reality TV turns once more. In Kelly's criticism of Wilson for "grandstanding," we hear an echo of Trump's supper-club vocabulary, as when he calls Comey a "showboat." In 2017, Kelly repeated the empty words of an empty man whose Midas touch turns everything not to gold, as Trump clearly wishes us to believe, but to whiteness (where Kelly himself is clearly quite comfortable). This is a step even Selina's Veep has not taken. That is how we know *VEEP* is fiction. And how the calumnious verities of Fox News are made real.

A year or two later, a news story would claim that Trump routinely refers to deceased and injured members of the U.S. military as "suckers" and "losers." In the *New Yorker*, John Cassidy would refer to the story as a "controversy" and call on John Kelly to settle it by saying "publicly what he knows." But it is not a "controversy." It is a well-reported and multiply confirmed story that the Administration denies. And John Kelly is not the one to settle it.

8

They Want Civility,
Let's Give It to Them

Grab 'em by the pussy. Reach over, she is right there, next to you on the plane, in your office, in the dressing room. There! For the TAKING! Lie, promise things you know you won't deliver, tell them how rich you are, or say you will get them a job on your show; whatever. Most yield, or perhaps it is just many who do. Or maybe just a few. (He exaggerates routinely, after all.) What if she says no? She won't say no! And if she does, so what? Who will know? Just say you tossed her first! Or call her a liar. Or, better: Demand an apology from her! Ha! That'll teach her. But what if later they complain? Then what? No problem: throw some money at 'em. "Here, don't say I never gave you anything." (He said that to Angela Merkel, Germany's chancellor, as he tossed a bag of candy at her at a G-7 meeting in June 2018.) What? You think that was rude? I was just JOKING! Can't you people take a joke?

He was joking, Marco Rubio will say a year later about Trump saying on the White House lawn that China should investigate the Bidens. I was just being sarcastic, Trump will say two years later about himself in 2020 when he was caught, spitballing in a pandemic, wondering out loud about whether bleach or light might help kill the coronavirus in the body. I was just teasing, says Gregory Anton in *Gaslight*, after he carefully puts in his wife's bag a trinket he plans to steal later in order to confuse her. "You might lose it. You know, you are inclined to lose things." "I am? I didn't realize that." "Just little things. I'll put it in your bag for safekeeping. There. Now, you'll remember where it is." "Don't be silly. Of course I'll remember." "I was teasing you, my dear."[1]

The owner of the Red Hen restaurant, in Lexington, Virginia, does not skate on civility's thin ice with "jokes," sarcasm, and teasing. She seems to be everything the president is not: serious, polite, civil, and well-intentioned. She risked her business out of respect for her workers who, like most restaurant workers, are among those on the presidential hit list since, as Anthony Bourdain's *Kitchen Confidential* made plain, the restaurant business is particularly hospitable to nonconforming people. Perhaps it is the melée of the kitchen that allows men—it is mostly men—who don't fit elsewhere to find a niche (though the niche is often a scene of exploitation too, as Bourdain knew).[2] In June 2018, informed that the president's press secretary, Sarah Huckabee Sanders, was dining in her restaurant that night, the Red Hen's owner consulted her employees, she did not tell them what to do; and then she represented them, she did not betray them. They objected on principle to serving Sanders, so the owner took the press secretary outside, presumably to save her embarrassment in front of others and to avoid a scene.

"I'm not a huge fan of confrontation," the Red Hen's Stephanie Wilkinson said later. But really, she had little choice. As Hannah Arendt notes, politics is not always something we choose to engage in. Sometimes politics comes to you and orders a cheese plate in your restaurant. That is when you are called upon to show who you are. Will you serve power, as power demands? Or show it the door?[3]

The desire in such moments to avoid a scene often leads to compliance. Not this time. Out on the porch, Wilkinson explained the press secretary would not be served dinner, refused her party's money, and asked her to leave. The press secretary left. (Note to country: if you refuse, they may comply.)

The story came out. The press secretary preened her moral superiority and said that, when asked to leave, she "politely left." As for the owner of the Red Hen? "Her actions," Sanders said, "say far more about her than about me. I always do my best to treat people, including those I disagree with, respectfully and will continue to do so." This last statement alone beggars all belief, given Sanders's almost daily barrage of snide prevarication from the podium at White House press briefings. But beggaring belief is surely the point. If Sanders and her boss could, they would make beggars of us all.

In a decent world, Stephanie Wilkinson's decency would shine like a beacon. Sanders was right that Wilkinson's actions said "more about her" than they did about Sanders. Wilkinson did not yell "fascist," she did not tweet out the press secretary's whereabouts and encourage a crowd to come protest her, she did not record their dinner conversation and release it to the press. These are all tactics others might have employed, and any of them might well be defensible in this political moment. But Wilkinson found her own way: she toed the line she could not cross, and she did so with civility. It seems to have done her no good. It has done her a world of good. It has done the world good.

Yes, she would soon have to resign her position as executive director of the downtown business association, part of the fallout of her stumble into public life. And her business had to close for a while because it was attacked by Sanders and by Trump, who tweeted a picture of the place and said, without evidence or reason, that the restaurant was unsanitary: "I always had a rule, if a restaurant is dirty on the outside, it is dirty on the inside!" He encouraged protests there, too. It was an outrageous use of executive power against a private citizen that has never been condemned as it should be.

But Maxine Waters, who has known from Day One who and what we are dealing with here, congratulated Wilkinson and called for more like her to step up. Waters called on all of us. Take courage from this example, she was saying. Take them out on the porch. Don't let it be business as usual. Don't just let it go. And now it is Waters, not the pussy-grabber, but the one who dares to call him what he is, who is told she should apologize. The audacity of civility is boundless. Power just loves to police the tone of its challengers, though, to be sure, the tone is not the only thing policed. A man who has always taken what he wants without asking now has at his behest the military, the Senate, and maybe the Supreme Court. With the full power of the U.S. government, his game is to see how far he can go. Our obligation is to stop him. No one tactic will do (VOTE!). No one else will do it (MOBILIZE!). One at a time and all together is the only way forward (RUN FOR OFFICE!).

Trump and his followers have put in their order. Let's not serve them. Every day they put on a show to distract us. Let's not let them. They tweet to raise the costs of resistance (fire the NFL players who kneel!). Let's not give in to them. Collective protests socialize those costs.

The aim is to discourage others from the kind of principled action taken by Stephanie Wilkinson. They know one refusal will inspire others. More importantly, their point is this: if no one is protesting, that must mean there is nothing to protest, just like when a nondisclosure agreement secures a woman's silence, and the conclusion we are told to accept is that the assault must not have happened. Or when tests are not given for a virus and therefore there are no cases. As Trump would say later, in May 2020 during the pandemic and then in Tulsa in June, "If we didn't do any testing, we would have very few cases."[4] Or if a police report doesn't mention eight shots fired by police into Breonna Taylor's body, then "we would have very few" police killings.

Stephanie Wilkinson's refusal has shone a light. Others have, too.

Just a few weeks after the Red Hen restaurant incident, Elin Ersson took it on herself to protest her country's deportation policy. "Early in the evening of July 23, 2018, a video is posted on Facebook. It is a close-up of a young woman with a flushed face, blonde hair, and dark-green glasses. Elin Ersson, 21, is walking up the aisle of a Turkish Airlines jet that is set to fly from Gothenburg to Istanbul. She is speaking English with a Swedish accent into her smartphone camera and livestreaming the scene on Facebook." Ersson refused to be seated, so the airplane she boarded could take off.[5]

Why? Because there is a man on the plane being deported from Sweden to Afghanistan, and his life is at stake. Standing alone in the aisle, streaming on Facebook, Ersson says, "I am not going to sit down until this person is off the plane." She is polite. But firm. The pilot has the right to refuse, too, she says, as the crew tries to persuade her into compliance. Passenger airline pilots are not obliged to be complicit in deportations. Meanwhile, a fellow passenger notes the deportation is perfectly legal: "Your country has rules." She does not dispute it: "I'm trying to change my country's rules," she replies. She knows she cannot do it alone: "As long as a person is standing up and if more people are standing up, then the pilot cannot take off."[6]

It is all very civil. After she explains the situation to a fellow passenger, he explains it to some others, and there is a smattering of applause. "We are with you," he says. And then, Ersson says, "the football team at the back is actually standing up. I want to salute them for standing up." She tears up. The mood of the cabin shifts a bit in her favor. Perhaps for this reason, a male passenger decides right then to take matters into his own hands. Can't she see she is frightening the children? he asks as he lunges for her phone. He wants the situation returned to normal, where young women like Ersson are compliant and men like him are in charge. But it doesn't work out that way. Not this time. His aggression only tilts the mood further in Ersson's direction. The crew returns her phone and sends him back to his seat. Soon she is told the deportee is being taken off the plane. Only after confirming the truth of that does she exit.

This is what Hannah Arendt calls action in concert. Someone has to start it. Others have to join. It requires courage and good fortune. For a full five to ten minutes, Ersson is in this by herself. It is really not clear which way things will go. The inconvenienced passengers could turn on her. Her reddening face betrays the difficulty of the situation. She tears up, first from the stress, and then with apparent gratitude when she finds that some of the passengers actually support her. Not all of them, but enough to tip the balance. That's all that is needed. Later, some would demand that charges be filed against her, and Ersson would be prosecuted for her actions. But though the prosecutor asked for a six-month sentence, she was only fined the equivalent of about 300 dollars.[7] I imagine it was worth it.

But the story is still more complicated. The man on the plane is not the one Ersson intended to rescue. Instead of the twenty-six-year-old being separated from his loving family in Sweden, on board the plane is a different Afghani man, in his fifties. The deportation of the twenty-six-year-old had been detoured to avoid interventions like Ersson's. "Taken by surprise, Ersson has to make a snap decision. Later, she says that she knew nothing about the [older] man, but that she was certain he was being deported to Afghanistan. 'So I decided to stand up for him,' she says."[8]

Her action did not go according to plan. Action rarely does. As Hannah Arendt says, we cannot control the parameters, effects, and consequences of political action. You might set out to save one man and end up saving another. Or none at all. That is why, Arendt says, forgiveness is a necessary feature of action. Without it, we would never risk acting politically, knowing it may go wrong and knowing *how* wrong it may go, even when we mean well. But Ersson does not ask for forgiveness, neither during her protest nor after. Perhaps this is because what Arendt saw as strength, the capacity to forgive, is now increasingly seen as weakness, an inability to stand strong. And forgiveness now is also gendered; these days it feminizes those who resort to asking for it. That is why gaslighters so often demand apologies from their victims; gaslighters weaponize forgiveness.

But Ersson does not second-guess herself. Not even when she is told that the man who was deplaned, thanks to her, has "a checkered past." He was no angel, U.S. newspapers would say. He was convicted in Sweden, sentenced to six months for beating his wife and daughters. Details like this could make a person question their principles. But Ersson has an admirable clarity to match her civility. "Nevertheless, he doesn't deserve to be deported to die back in Afghanistan," she says. Deportation to Afghanistan is no different from a death penalty, she says, and "the abolition of the death penalty was a major achievement for Swedish law."[9] Are they now outsourcing what they proudly abolished? Anyway, there are messy details on all sides. Why don't the messy details of Sweden's refugee policy, the suicides, the riven families, and the ruined lives, why don't these messy details lead defenders of deportation to question *their* commitments?

It is important to feminist criticism that Ersson's clarity, civility, and power are grounded in her experience living and protesting with refugees seeking asylum in Sweden. If she does not easily lose her bearings, it is because she embeds herself in a plurality that confirms the knowledge of her senses. And she is rooted, she says, in her Swedish upbringing, which valued tolerance and treated it as common sense. She listens to the claims made by asylum-seekers. She joins with them in public protests. She does not hesitate to hug their family members. She is with them.

In her own way, Stephanie Wilkinson of the Red Hen restaurant did something similar. She stood with her staff and acknowledged the costs of her choice. "I have a business, and I want the business to thrive." But that business consists of a chef, managers, and wait staff currently under threat. Several are gay, and they "knew Sanders had defended Trump's desire to bar transgender people from the military. This month, they had all watched her evade questions and defend a Trump policy that caused migrant children to be separated from their parents."[10] On the night Sanders turned up in their restaurant expecting to be served, the staff called Wilkinson at home. She came right over. They talked to her. She listened. "Tell me what you want me to do. I can ask her to leave." That is what the staff wanted, and Wilkinson acted accordingly. "This feels like the moment in our democracy when people have to make uncomfortable actions and decisions to uphold their morals," she says. It matters who is welcomed in and who is cast out of our circles of belonging, and why. And, if it also matters how it is done, then we can note that in both these cases it was all very civil.

9

Stormy Daniels's #MeToo Moment

"A guy walked up on me and said to me, 'Leave Trump alone. Forget the story,'" Stormy Daniels told Anderson Cooper on *60 Minutes* on March 25, 2018.[1] Back then, it was 2011, and she was in a parking lot. Her baby was in the car seat, and she was on her way to the gym. The man then "leaned around and looked at my daughter and said, 'That's a beautiful little girl. It'd be a shame if something happened to her mom.'" The scene is straight out of one of those movies where nothing good happens to women in parking lots, and the words "It'd be a shame if . . ." are downright terrifying. Such a threat would stay with a person and might shape their decisions for a long time to come. Daniels was, she says, "rattled."

Five years later, when on the eve of the 2016 U.S. presidential election Daniels signed a nondisclosure agreement and then made some statements denying she had ever had sex with Trump, there was no explicit threat of physical violence, but Daniels was again intimidated. "The exact sentence used was, 'They can make your life hell in many different ways,'" she told Anderson Cooper.

Regarding these two experiences, Daniels is willing to say she felt she had no choice. Why then does she offer such a different account of the events that took place in a hotel room in Lake Tahoe in 2006, where, by her own account, she felt pressured to have sex with Trump and also felt she had no choice? It was her own fault, she says: "I realized exactly what I'd gotten myself into. And I was like, 'Ugh, here we go.' (LAUGH) And I just felt like maybe—(LAUGH) it was sort of—I had it coming for making a bad decision for going to someone's room alone and I just heard the voice in my head, 'well, you put yourself in a bad situation and bad things happen, so you deserve this.'"

The bad thing was sex with Trump. The voice in her head that told her she deserved it? That was her #MeToo moment.

She had gone to dinner with a wealthy, powerful man, hoping to get ahead. She was not attracted to him. When she went to the bathroom, he moved from the dining table to the bedroom. When she returned, she found him "perched" on

the bed. His body language was clear. She even imitated it during the interview, miming with her body the open torso of male expectation.

> ANDERSON COOPER: Did you view it as: "This is
> a potential opportunity. I'm gonna see where
> it goes?"
> STORMY DANIELS: I thought of it as a business deal.

Trump had lured Daniels with Harvey Weinstein–style promises. At dinner, he said, "Got an idea, honeybunch. Would you ever consider going on and—and being a contestant?"[2] On *Celebrity Apprentice,* he meant. "And I laughed and—and said, 'NBC's never gonna let, you know, an adult film star be on.'" On the contrary, he reassured her: "That's why I want you. You're gonna shock a lotta people, you're smart and they won't know what to expect."

He knew what he expected, though.

> ANDERSON COOPER: And you had sex with him.
> STORMY DANIELS: Yes.

She says she didn't want to; but she rejects the #MeToo label. She did it of her own volition, she insists, unlike the "true victims" in the #MeToo movement who were raped or coerced. Her concern for the other women is laudable. But it misses the point: the offenses against women charted by #MeToo range from outright sexual violence to coercion to pressure to quid pro quo.

Did Daniels comply because she worried about what might happen if she didn't? Did she not want to risk making a scene? Or losing out on a job she wanted, that he had said she was right for? Many women will recognize the #MeToo calculation. It is easier to relent to the known than to refuse and have to court the unknown: his anger, his disappointment, perhaps his vengeance. Many women who make those calculations also seek to own their choices, constrained as they are, so that they will not be seen as "victims." Nobody wants to be a victim.

A *Washington Post* article about Daniels puts her in the context of powerful women in the adult film industry. Daniels is impressive, unblinking in the media spotlight, and self-possessed. But that doesn't mean she could totally burn the standard script of misogyny, nor does it mean she had the power fully to rewrite her role in it. The #MeToo movement calls attention to the scripts that are foisted upon us while we nonetheless assume we are responsible for them: the ones that oblige and then silence women, while falsely promising all sorts of opportunities or rewards.

We need not call her a victim or a survivor in order to see that the power that had earlier that evening allowed Daniels to pick up a magazine and playfully spank this man out of his self-regard was momentary and had in any case been granted to her as a noblesse oblige. In patriarchy, women with spunk are allowed to spank men who enjoy the temporary release from having to be powerful *all* the time. For the men, it is just role-play. But the women are played by the role; and sometimes they are left rattled.

Does it matter that Daniels was in that hotel room hoping to advance her career? Yes, it matters, but not in a way that leads to her undoing. How many men have had dinner with potential employers—seeking professional advancement—without fear of such extortion?

Daniels says she *knew* Trump wasn't going to deliver on his promises. She was way too savvy to fall for that, she says. But she lets her hope show for a second, and anyone moved by #MeToo should be moved by this, too. She says that Trump later called to say he "just wanted to give [her] a quick update, we had a meeting, it went great . . . [and] they're totally into the idea." He was suggesting she would get her shot on his show. Her response, she says, "was like 'mhmm,'" and she adds, "That part I never believed." But when Anderson Cooper asks, "Did you still get the sense that he was kind of dangling it in front of you . . . to keep you interested, to keep you coming back?" Daniels replies, "Of course, of course. I mean, I'm not blind. But at the same time, maybe it'll work out, you know?"

Her cynical knowingness ("I mean, I'm not blind"), which makes her *not* a victim, does not quite extinguish the still faintly hopeful optimism ("maybe it'll work out, you know?") that makes her, if not a victim, then a casualty of the misogyny #MeToo condemns. If she thought she deserved what she was getting that first night in Tahoe, it was not simply because she had made the bad call to go for dinner "to someone's room alone." It was surely because she allowed herself to go to that dinner hopeful. She thought maybe she could get out of pornography and onto the *Celebrity Apprentice* (that fifty shades of upward mobility that can make quite a difference). And her hope was dashed. Rather than her abusing his desire, by refusing him, he abused hers as he used the illusion of consent to maneuver her onto a casting couch for a role that did not exist and never would.

When Daniels then says to Anderson Cooper, "I was not a victim. I've never said I was a victim," she may be recalling her second meeting with Trump, a year later. This time they met in Trump's Beverly Hills Hotel bungalow, and Daniels flipped the script. When Trump approached her for sex, four hours after she arrived, she said, "'Well, before, you know, can we talk about what's the development?' And he was like, 'I'm almost there. I'll have an answer for you next week.' And I was like, 'Okay, cool. Well—I guess call me next week.' And I just took my purse and left."

Alyssa Rosenberg rightly notes in the *Washington Post* that "as a cultural milestone, the most radical thing Cooper did was refuse to treat [Daniels] as if she was irresponsible or immoral, or as if she were less than credible simply because of what she does for a living."[3] He did not shame her or suggest that her job—which is legal—made her less credible. But he did miss one big opportunity when asking her about that first meeting with Trump in Tahoe:

> ANDERSON COOPER: And you had sex with him.
>
> STORMY DANIELS: Yes.
>
> ANDERSON COOPER: You were 27, he was 60. Were you physically attracted to him?
>
> STORMY DANIELS: No.
>
> ANDERSON COOPER: Not at all?
>
> STORMY DANIELS: No.
>
> ANDERSON COOPER: Did you want to have sex with him?
>
> STORMY DANIELS: No. But I didn't—I didn't say no. I'm not a victim, I'm not—
>
> ANDERSON COOPER: It was entirely consensual.
>
> STORMY DANIELS: Oh, yes, yes.

Cooper's "It was entirely consensual" does not match the event described. And Daniels's "Oh, yes, yes" is a clue that should not be overlooked: it literally doubles down on her insistence she is not a victim, while also sounding the trite refrain of faked orgasms heard round the world.

10

The Trump Doctrine

In a 1994 interview with ABC News's Nancy Collins, Trump said, "Psychologists will tell you that some women want to be treated with respect, others differently. I tell friends who treat their wives magnificently, get treated like crap in return, 'Be rougher and you'll see a different relationship.'"[1] If there is a Trump Doctrine, that is it. U.S. allies are now, structurally, the "wife." In 2019, that went double for Germany's Angela Merkel and then prime minister of the U.K. Theresa May.

Later, in 2020, it would go triple for Andrew Cuomo and New York State. "It's a two-way street," Trump said of distributing tax dollars to states struggling to respond to the coronavirus pandemic. "They have to treat us well, too," he said, reprising his Ukraine move ("do us a favor though") in which government support and policy implementation depend on how he is treated and whether he gets what he wants.

The Trump Doctrine, such as it is, applies not just to America's allies and not just to governors, but also to the

American public. We are the wife, too. And it is an abusive
relationship, as several commentators have pointed out: we
are showered with praise one day, then thrown off-balance
by strange behaviors or pummeled with rage the next. Jessica Winter argues that "the language of the Trump administration is the language of domestic violence."[2] And Leah
MacElrath tweeted, "Just as abusers isolate victims from
their friends/family, Trump is isolating the United States
from its allies. Isolation feeds an abuser's false narrative of
'you have no friends/no one loves you like I do' and gives the
abuser greater psychological control."[3] Earlier on, during the
2016 campaign, Kendra Lubalin listed the signs of abuse
provided by the National Domestic Violence Hotline—gaslighting, manipulating, isolating the partner, and victim
blaming—alongside evidence of each pulled from stories of
the day.[4] To Lubalin's evidence of victim blaming, we could
add the July 2018 charge by Trump that "D.N.C. should be
ashamed of themselves for allowing themselves to be
hacked."[5] Most eerily prescient on Lubalin's list is "threatening to harm or take away your children," since thousands of
children have now been separated from their families at the
U.S./Mexico border, the U.S.'s new Guantanamo. Lubalin
also noted that when Trump talked about fighting terrorism,
"he said waterboarding wasn't 'tough enough' and we needed
to get behind torture that is almost 'unthinkable.'"[6]

Trump's advice—to use torture, to do the unthinkable,
and to be rougher—calls to mind Machiavelli's misogynistic
counsel in The Prince, his book of advice to princes. Fortuna, Machiavelli says, referring to the lucky break or chance
contingency that will make or break a man of action, "is a
woman, and if you wish to keep her under it is necessary to
beat and ill-use her." If opportunity knocks, you need to
knock her back. Fortuna is the prince's frenemy, and the
prince who wants to succeed must be willing forcibly to

bend Fortuna to his will. Grab her by the pussy, Machiavelli all but says. Hesitate and you're a loser: "She allows herself to be mastered by the adventurous rather than by those who go to work more coldly." But she is unpredictable and powerful. Those who try to grab hold of Fortuna take their chances.[7]

Centuries later, Machiavelli's misogyny is alive and well. The *New York Times* recently reported on domestic abusers who use the new twenty-first-century tools of smart homes to control and intimidate their partners. Some women are isolated in their homes by tormenters who monitor their every move. Others are locked out. One woman had turned on her air-conditioner, but it then switched off without her touching it. Another said the code numbers of her front door's digital lock changed every day, and she could not figure out why. Still another told an abuse help line that she kept hearing the doorbell ring, but no one was there.[8] It is as if Gregory Anton from *Gaslight* had found his way to Hammacher Schlemmer and used his wife's credit card to buy up all the latest gadgets.

When one women's advocate says, "They feel like they're losing control of their home," a lot of us know the feeling.[9] These incidents exemplify the household level of patriarchy, but they also magnify our national predicament. We can all empathize with the sense of confusion when locks are changed without notice (asylum-seekers suddenly subjected to a new, inhumane policy of so-called zero tolerance) or doorbells ring but no one is there (those phantom immigrants supposedly sneaking in at the border), lights go on and off without reason (blackouts in Puerto Rico), and temperature changes weirdly (climate change means snow in May and record-high temperatures in January).

The new technology amplifies and extends old, familiar practices of domination. It seems Trump has control of the whole damned house at his fingertips, but that is no reason to give up. As Machiavelli notes, "He who becomes master of a city used to being free and does not destroy her can expect to be destroyed by her."[10] Sure enough, by 2018, civil society is fighting back, shunning members of the Trump administration who daily lie and dissemble on behalf of a cruel agenda that violates international and national laws of asylum, basic human rights, decency, and much more. Huckabee Sanders, Kirstjen Nielsen, Mitch McConnell, and Stephen Miller have all been chased from restaurants. Scott Pruitt was confronted, mid-lunch, by a woman named Kristin Mink. Holding her two-year-old in her arms, Mink said her son and all of us deserve to have someone at the EPA who really looks out for the environment. She urged Pruitt to "resign before your scandals push you out." Resign now, she said. Two days later, Scott Pruitt resigned. Perhaps Fortuna really is a woman, after all.

But not all women are Fortuna. Many act more like the free citizens of the free republics Machiavelli admired. Such women build organizations to support others, rather than just trusting their fates to a sudden surprise that may break in their favor. Some volunteer to answer the phones at the National Domestic Violence Hotline. Trained to know the signs of abuse, they can confirm the evidence of the callers' senses. Volunteers and trainers know the importance of infrastructure and community to the healing of women subjected to this sort of violence. They also mobilize women to run for office, or vote, or represent victims in court. Many work with Black Lives Matter to call attention to police violence against Black women, which somehow never gets the same attention as that against Black men, perhaps partly because so much of the violence against women occurs inside the home (as in the case of Breonna Taylor, awakened then killed by police in March 2020 with a so-called no-knock warrant). Altogether, the work is to change society's defaults from "pay attention to men" to "pay attention to women," from "believe men" to "believe women."

When the default is to believe men, it is uncontroversial to ask, as MSNBC's Chris Matthews did of Elizabeth Warren in 2020, "But why would he lie? What reason does he have to lie?" The "he" was Mike Bloomberg, and Warren had in that evening's Democratic Party primary debate said that she believed the women who claimed they have been harassed or treated inequitably when they worked for Bloomberg. Matthews was dubious for no particular reason. He was just still operating by the old default. The old default believes Mike. The new default asks, no less rhetorically, but why would *she* lie? What reason does *she* have to lie? This was Warren's response to Matthews that night.

"Believe women" is the slogan of the #MeToo movement not because we should believe *all* women, but because we need to switch the default from the misogynistic habit of doubting women to believing them.[11] Matthews lost his job over his exchange with Warren, which outraged many, but that alone is not enough to switch the defaults. It is time for feminists to take away the keys and change the codes of those who cannot imagine and do not support true sex-gender and racial equality. Voting is a key part of the picture, a powerfully necessary way to insist on our own sets of keys and codes. After all, it's our house, too.

11

Jon Stewart and the Limits of Mockery

These days, midway through Trump's (first?) term, I find myself feeling like Faye Dunaway in *Chinatown* when Jack Nicholson slaps her face demanding the truth about the identity of a young woman she cares for, and Faye Dunaway cries, "She's my sister, my daughter, my sister, my daughter. . . ." In my own waking nightmare version of this scene, reality slaps me in the face, demanding to know who Trump is, and I cry, "He's Reagan! He's Hitler. He's Reagan. He's Hitler." Mindful that the world is at stake, I call it my Chinatown Syndrome.[1]

In both *Chinatown*, the movie, and in the U.S. in 2018, it is unclear whether a wealthy, belligerent character is just a regular aggressive, racist man who pushes people around to get his way or an exceptionally immoral one who will murder, rape, and plunder without hesitation in order to remake the world to his liking. Which is it? Early on in the course of events, it can be hard to know. As in an abusive relationship, the truth of such things often creeps up on you. That is why domestic abuse centers share signs of "early warning."

I know, I know: Reagan was no Hitler. But that didn't stop the Klan from endorsing him. And it didn't stop Reagan from making an official visit in 1985 to a cemetery in Bitburg, Germany, where WWII German military *and* SS members were buried. The visit was to commemorate the fortieth anniversary of the end of WWII, but there were protests against Reagan paying respects to SS war dead. Reagan defended his visit: "These [SS troops] were the villains, as we know, that conducted the persecutions and all. But there are 2,000 graves there, and most of those, the average age is about 18," many of them drafted and so "they were victims, just as surely as the victims in the concentration camps." There were victims on both sides.

Elie Wiesel, the Holocaust survivor and author, tried to stop Reagan's visit: I "implore you," he said, "to do something else, to find another way, another site. That place, Mr. President, is not your place."[2] Except maybe it *was* his place. Reagan, who had been governor of California, began his first presidential campaign in 1980 with a states' rights speech in Mississippi's Neshoba County Fair—the same county where in 1964 civil rights workers Andrew Goodman, Michael Schwerner, and James Chaney were murdered. There was a message in that. The Klan got it.[3] The same message informed Trump's 2020 decision to hold his first rally since Covid-19 in Tulsa, Oklahoma, famous for its horrifying massacre, which destroyed Tulsa's famous "Black Wall Street," and dispossessed hundreds of African Americans in 1921.

In 1985 Wiesel called Reagan "Mr. President," seeking to elevate Reagan to the height of the office. But imploring didn't work for Wiesel with Reagan, nor for Rock Hudson, who also implored but was ignored by that same White House when, dying of AIDS, he asked his old Hollywood friends, the Reagans, to help. They did not take his calls.

In a brilliant eight-minute appearance on *The Late Show with Stephen Colbert*, in July 2018, Jon Stewart followed in Wiesel's footsteps, but he tried a different tactic.[4] Imploring feeds and flatters the power one seeks to undo. You might get the favor, but you have added to their power, and now you are in debt, too. Stewart tried something else.

Rather than implore, Stewart mocks. Although Stewart starts his eight minutes by underlining his own seeming powerlessness, his intention is not to stay there but to reject efforts by the powerful to put good people of conscience in their place. He opens with a nervous titter and says, somewhat cartoonishly, "Hello Donald, it's me!" And then, haltingly, "The guy you made sure everyone knew was Jewish on Twitter." Trump's outing of him as a Jew (no secret) had happened years earlier, but citing it now, Stewart gives quick, specific context to Trump's current cruelties at the border, his support for and from neo-Nazis and white supremacists, his white nationalist anti-integrationism, his administration's move to denationalize naturalized citizens not just in response to legal complaints, as used to be the case, but proactively, and its new abrogation of agreements with foreign-born soldiers to fast-track their citizenship—all measures disturbingly reminiscent of Nazi denationalization policies in 1930s Germany.[5]

Stewart can risk the position of Jewish powerlessness— "the guy" who was outed on Twitter—because he will go on to ironize it. He begins in earnest: "If there's one hallmark to your presidency that I think we're finding the most difficult," he says, as if he could move Trump to care about that, "it is that no matter what you do"—and here the gear shifts from plaintive to mocking—"it always comes with an extra layer of gleeful cruelty. And dickish-ness." Stewart then slips back into earnestness, closer to Wiesel's mode: "Donald, you could have absolutely made a more stringent border policy, and have made your point about enforcement, but I guess it wouldn't have felt right without a Dickensian level of villainy. You casually separated people seeking asylum from their children. From babies. It made me realize something . . ."—and now we see the earnestness was a set-up: "You may be orange, you may like hamburgers, you may be a clown. But you are no Ronald McDonald." Indeed, given Trump's penchant for hamburgers and getting things for free (as numerous contractors attest), he lines up best with Ronald McDonald's foe, the Hamburglar, who craves burgers and steals them (and is invariably caught).

Stewart's joke is subtle but brilliant, because Ronald McDonald is not just any clown, but a mascot, not only for McDonald's, the fast food chain Trump favors, but for the charity it founded to support families whose children are in hospital. Its tag line? *"Keeping families with sick children together and near the care and resources they need."*[6]

And then Stewart shifts gears one more time. Why? Because mocking and imploring have too much in common: no matter how bravely performed, the shadow of subservience is discernible in both. So Stewart draws a new circle of belonging around those who join him in rejecting new border policies and naming them evil. Showing clips of Fox News talking heads and of Sarah Huckabee Sanders calling Trump a true leader for the crimes at the border, Stewart says, "Clearly we are not going to be able to negotiate or shame you into decency but there is one place where I draw the line; I won't allow you and your sycophants to turn cruelty into virtue." He cites Abraham Lincoln, who said that those who defended slavery had just one demand: "Cease to call slavery wrong and join them in calling it right." Lincoln refused to yield to this demand. That refusal is a marker of what the political theorist George Kateb calls democratic individuality.

It is in order to break down what is left of democratic individuality that Trump, at a Montana rally in July 2018, insulted George H. W. Bush's Republican presidential campaign slogan from 1988: a "thousand points of light." Trump crowed to his audience that day that people everywhere "get" the meaning of *his* slogans, "Make America Great Again" and "Putting America First." But not "Thousand Points of Light." He said with his characteristic smirk, "'Thousand Points of Light,' I never quite got that one. What the hell is that? Has anyone ever figured that one out? And it was put by a Republican, wasn't it?"

It was. Trump's mockery of the slogan is not just a move to extend his domination of the Bush I remnants of the Republican Party. The joke not only mocked Bush Sr., who was always too patrician, even for the 1980s Republican base. It also mocked the very idea of people serving as points of light in the darkness. The aim is to diminish the Stephanie Wilkinsons, Elin Erssons, Frederica Wilsons, Kristin Minkses, Maxine Waterses, and the Jon Stewarts who step out and show the way. The very serious message of Jon Stewart's eight minutes is that this is the issue now, to join together as a thousand points of fight. His gift is his clarity about what is at stake. It is a point of orientation in a miasma of disinformation and distraction, like a gaslight that still lights the way, even if it flickers mysteriously.

12

Bullying Canada

An American Presidential Tradition

On his first reality TV show, *The Apprentice*, Trump said to a young woman on the show, a contestant, "Must be a pretty picture, you dropping to your knees."

A bent knee is what American presidents have always expected from the U.S.'s close ally, Canada. This is worth noting because an assault on Canada in June 2018 was one of the many moments that year when Trump's actions as president were greeted with shock and outrage.[1] To be clear, it is absolutely necessary to feel outrage in response to violations of human rights and to express shock at policies that are discriminatory, corrupt, and evil. Hundreds, perhaps thousands of children—no one knows how many because no one in government bothered to keep track—were separated from their parents at the border and are still separated from their families. But our outrage also confirms Trump's followers' sense that he is really shaking things up and *that* is what they love about him. The more outraged we are, the more he must be *right for them*. If "owning the libs" is the endgame, then our outrage always falls into the trap of Trump's version of shock politics. And yet, often, it should be noted, outrage is generated by actions that are not really a shake-up at all, more in keeping with the past than a break from it.

Consider the case of U.S.-Canada relations. After leaving the June 2018 G7 meeting in Quebec, Trump got into a Twitter spat with Prime Minister Justin Trudeau, charging that Trudeau was appropriately "meek and mild" during their meeting and then "dishonest" about it after Trump left. What melodrama. Most Americans watched agog: Canada? We are falling out with Canada? But Canadians are so nice! And it is true. What is not true, however, is that U.S.-Canada relations are always copacetic. Here are just a few examples from a long history.

In the early 1960s, when both countries were working out a still new joint defense agreement called NORAD (North American Defense), John F. Kennedy expected compliance, but Canadian prime minister John Diefenbaker would not provide it.

In 1961, after the Bay of Pigs fiasco, Kennedy made a state visit to Canada seeking rehabilitation. (Canada, it seems, is the Betty Ford Center of flailing U.S. presidents.[2]) Kennedy spoke to Parliament and joked about Diefenbaker's bad French, perhaps not realizing the linguistic sensitivities in the Canadian context. There were several more intended or unintended insults, all leading up to a fateful day over a year later, in October 1962, when Kennedy called Diefenbaker to tell him there were Russian bases in Cuba, and the U.S. would need Canada's military and naval support to respond. The Canadian prime minister said he could not grant the American request without seeing better pictures. The ones brought by U.S. emissaries had been grainy and entirely unclear, he explained. Kennedy was livid and angrily hung up on his Canadian counterpart. (Remember when, in his first month in office, Trump hung up on his Australian counterpart, then prime minister Malcolm Turnbull? "*Unprecedented!*," people cried.)

Kennedy had already been working to replace Diefenbaker with Canada's leader of the opposition, Lester B. Pearson, because, from the beginning of Kennedy's term, Diefenbaker resisted U.S. demands that Canada nuclearize its defense as part of its NORAD commitments. Diefenbaker deferred and delayed. He was not indecisive; he was canny. Kennedy knew Pearson would be a more cooperative partner.

So, for Canada's 1962 and 1963 elections, Kennedy sent his pollster Lou Harris to Canada to work closely and secretly with Pearson. Fifty years later, Lou Harris said, "One of the highlights of my life was helping Pearson defeat Diefenbaker." McGeorge Bundy would also brag about having brought down Diefenbaker's government. Bundy likely knew all the details that later came to light: the U.S. embassy in Ottawa leaked anti-Diefenbaker stories to the media, the White House issued statements undercutting Diefenbaker's defense-policy positions, and an unflattering cover story about the prime minister published in *Newsweek* was shepherded into print by political editor and friend of Kennedy Ben Bradlee. Bradlee would later joke that, contrary to published reports, Kennedy didn't think Diefenbaker was an S.O.B. No, "he thought he was a prick."[3]

In April 1962, during the lead-up to the first of two Canadian elections that would be held during Kennedy's time in office—in June 1962 and April 1963—Kennedy hosted a White House dinner for American Nobel Laureates and invited Pearson, a 1957 Nobel Laureate for his work to resolve the Suez Crisis, but not an American. Nonetheless, he was there and was given pride of place: seated at Jackie's table at the dinner, his own wife seated at the president's. The event was widely covered, and Canadians were not immune to the cool of the Kennedys' Camelot.[4] A year later, in 1963, Pearson defeated Diefenbaker to become prime minister of Canada, and Pearson agreed to nuclearize Canada's defense. (This policy change was undone just a few years later by the next prime minister from the same party as Pearson: Pierre Elliot Trudeau, a.k.a. Justin's father.)

By 1965, Lyndon Johnson was in office in the U.S., and Pearson was a bit less compliant (it happens, sometimes, with client states). Pearson gave a speech in the U.S., at Temple University, criticizing America's Vietnam War and calling on Johnson to halt the bombing unilaterally and seek a negotiated settlement with the Democratic Republic of Vietnam. Before Pearson finished his speech, he was summoned to Camp David, where Johnson grabbed Pearson by the lapels, lifted him up bodily, and shouted, "Don't you come into my living room and piss on my rug." It was vintage Johnson, but Kennedy would surely have done much the same. Actually, we now know, he did far more.

It was the same with the next president and prime minister. After a meeting with Pierre Elliot Trudeau, Richard Nixon said to Bob Haldeman, "You've got to put it to these people for kicking the U.S. around. . . . Give it to somebody here" (by which he meant, plant a negative story about Trudeau with journalist Jack Anderson).[5] When it was later reported that Nixon called Trudeau an "asshole" and Trudeau was asked to respond, he said, "I've been called worse things by better people." Score one for the Canadians.

So now, forty-odd years later, Trump tweets that Trudeau *fils* is disloyal and weak. Shocking? Unprecedented? It seems rather mild in light of this history. Indeed, with this history in mind, we may notice something: after Trump's Twitter spat, there was suddenly some reporting on some old #MeToo-style charges against Justin Trudeau.[6] At roughly the same time, Stephen Harper, Canada's leader of the opposition, was visiting Trump in Washington, D.C. Was this one more effort by the U.S. to use the media to bring about a change in Canada's leadership? We may not ever know for sure, but we do know this: within a year Trudeau would go on to lose his majority in Parliament, and this is exactly what happened to Diefenbaker in '62, before he and the Conservatives finally lost governance power entirely in '63, and remained the minority party in Parliament for almost two decades thereafter.[7] History rhymes, but it doesn't quite repeat: American demands on Canada now seem unlikely to include nuclearization for joint defense against Russia.

Head of state relationships can be mercurial, and they make for good stories, but the day-to-day operations of U.S./Canadian bureaucratic machinery are functionally bilateral and solid. Indeed, that smooth working machinery may have been precisely what set Trump off on Trudeau. Perhaps someone told Trump what political scientist Christopher Sands reports: "Canada's strategy with Trump [up until the 2018 G7 meeting] has been 'brilliant' . . . focus[ed] on court- ing municipal, state and congressional leaders in order to push a data-focused, pro-free trade approach to NAFTA."[8] Political scientists prefer to focus on institutions because that is where they think the real action is. But which institu- tion? In his 1961 speech to the Canadian Parliament, Ken- nedy highlighted one not normally treated as political.

"Geography has made us neighbors. History has made us friends. Economics has made us partners. And necessity has made us allies. Those whom nature hath so joined together, let no man put asunder."

That last line got a laugh as well as applause: "let no man put asunder" is from Matthew 19:6 on the impermissibility of divorce. The joke suggests that to understand Canada- U.S. relations will require not just attention to institutions like municipalities but also to marriage and, further, to structure, like *patriarchy*.

American presidents expect wifely submission from the neighbor to the North, and this gendered expectation is not restricted to Canada. Anyone can be made "the woman" in an abusive relationship. Just ask James Comey.[9] Or France. From Kennedy to Nixon to Reagan and beyond, Trump has stepped into an office in which his views on Canada, as well as his views on race and gender, are for the most part quite comfortable.

What *is* unprecedented is the opportunity this moment may provide for radical change in the United States. Genuinely new possibilities require, however, that we insist on what Trump himself insists on but some Republicans don't: that he and the party of Reagan *are* one.[10] A 2018 *New York Times* op-ed by an anonymous "senior official in the Trump administration" about so-called resistance inside the White House is a first move in what will soon be a large-scale effort to wriggle out of that one.[11] There will be many more when the ship starts sinking. Right now, some of those on board can feel the ship begin to list. No wonder they call it "leaking."

13

House Renovations

For Christine Blasey Ford

One thing that sent Christine Blasey Ford to therapy in 2012 was a marital disagreement about a house renovation. Such renovations create the kind of conflict that can really test a marriage: this is the trite premise of many HGTV design shows. But the story Blasey Ford told was anything but trite. Against the advice of an architect and against the wishes of her husband, she was insisting on two front doors for their renovated house. Two front doors? The architect and the husband objected, but she would not yield. So off to therapy she and her husband went. It was there that the feelings that drove her insistence surfaced. Fittingly, almost poetically, the battle over the doors to her home opened the door to her trauma. She told her story in therapy back then, and, this week, she told it again, in detail, to the nation.

She had been attacked when she was fifteen, thrown against her will into a bedroom by two seventeen-year-old boys, immobilized on a bed by one, Brett Kavanaugh, who groped her, pressed his body against hers, and tried to remove her clothes. When she screamed for help, he clapped his hand over her mouth to silence her, and this made her fear for her life. At the Senate hearings into Kavanaugh's nomination to a seat on the Supreme Court, Blasey Ford was asked what specifically she remembered about that day, and she said she was haunted by the laughter between the boys and by the moment when she appealed with her eyes to the second boy for help, only to realize he would not intervene.

She also mentioned but did not dwell on another detail. Once inside, the boys locked the door of the room into which they threw her. When she found an opportunity to escape, she dashed from the bedroom to a bathroom across the hall, locked herself in there, and waited. How long? We do not know. After a time, the boys left the bedroom, and she heard them, as she so memorably put it, "pinballing" down the stairs. She must have been listening hard, straining to track their movements, trying to decipher the sounds and infer their meaning from behind the locked bathroom door. She was not yet out of trouble, after all; she was locked in a bathroom, hiding. She heard her attackers talking and laughing with each other on the stairs, and then she heard the noise of a larger conversation, as the boys rejoined the social gathering. Here is where I imagine she must have spent some time calculating. Was it safe yet to try to escape? Had she waited long enough? Were her attackers now otherwise engaged? Distracted by drinking and hanging around with their friends? Were they far enough from the front door that she could get by them and make it safely out of the house? What courage it must have taken her to open that locked bathroom door, risk the descent down the stairs, and then the dash out the front door to the street. She did not mention such details at the hearing. She may not remember. But she recalled in her statement her relief as she realized, once she was outside, that the two boys were not coming after her. That says it all.

So does her story of happening on one of her attackers at the Safeway grocery store a few weeks later. Here, too, doors play a role. In answer to questions from Rachel Mitchell, the female prosecuting attorney hired by Senate Republicans for the occasion, Blasey Ford explained there were multiple entrances to the Safeway store, and that when her mother chose one, Blasey Ford, a teenager wanting her independence, chose another. Ironically, the one she chose was *not* the safe way. The Safeway door she went through put her face to face with Mark Judge, the other of the two boys who had attacked her. Blasey Ford said hi, as they had done in the past, before the attack. Judge seemed nervous and uncomfortable, she recalls. Somehow in her testimony, she recalled his feelings, not hers.

So much of what happens in our lives depends on the doors that appear before us, or not, on which ones we choose to go through and which we pass by. On "Let's Make a Deal," the TV game show with the Trumpian name, contestants must choose Door Number One, Two, or Three. The game show teaches that our fate depends on our free choice, and this means that we deserve what we get. We chose it! But it is a poor, even cruel lesson because, in the United States, some people walk breezily through doors that seem magically to open for them, while others jiggle handles that will not turn, and still others search in vain for just a threshold on which to stand. Brett Kavanaugh said at the hearings for his Supreme Court appointment that he had no connections at Yale and got there only by dint of his very hard work in high school (a claim belied by numerous accounts of his hard drinking at the time), as if the doors to Yale were not opened for him by his school, the exclusive and well-connected Georgetown Prep, or by his mother, the judge, and his father, the lobbyist. For some, it seems, all the doors are the safe way. For others, it seems, none are. Some of us are told we are free to head this way or that, only to suddenly find ourselves thrust into rooms locked behind us. For many others in our racially riven and radically unequal society, the only doors that seem to open are doors of no return, prison doors, locked, with keys thrown away for years, maybe forever.

I thought of all these doors as I watched two women, activists at the Capitol as part of a protest, stand in an elevator doorway and reproach Senator Jeff Flake the day after Blasey Ford's testimony. Flake had announced his intention to vote in favor of Brett Kavanaugh's appointment to the Supreme Court. Ana Maria Archila and Maria Gallagher, both survivors of sexual assault, asked the senator: did their suffering mean nothing? If men who attack women are promoted, what does that mean about how society values women?

Scholars of immigration politics see elevator behavior as a useful metaphor. When you get on an elevator and someone down the hall calls "Wait!," *do* you wait? Or do you quietly hit the button so the door closes and you are on your solitary way? What you do in this context may predict your views on immigration. With the cameras on him, Jeff Flake looked like he was keeping the door open for those two women who stood on its threshold and made their appeal. The women spoke and demanded that Flake listen. "Look at me when I am talking to you," one said. And he did.

The video of their encounter went viral, and Flake, in response, changed his position slightly, breaking ranks to ask that the background investigation into Kavanaugh be reopened. In the end, it would not make a difference. It was designed to not make a difference, performed hastily and constrained to prevent anything from turning up.[1] It was more for show than anything else. But still, on *Fox News* that night, Laura Ingraham wondered, *What is wrong with Flake's staff? Why didn't they call the Capitol Police, she asked, and have those women taken away?* For what? It was surely a politically uncomfortable moment for Flake, who was literally cornered in that elevator. But he was not in fear for his safety. No one threw her body on top of his and muzzled his mouth. What would the police have arrested Archila and Gallagher for? Practicing citizenship?

The two women in the elevator doorway were inspired by Blasey Ford, who showed them a second door where they had thought there was only one, closed to survivors like them. Archila said, "It was Dr. Ford's story that allowed me to tell this secret to my parents. I now have to do the work of how me and my parents process the experience, and I don't know how this is going to go." She chose to walk through a new doorway without knowing for sure where it would lead. That takes courage.

Because of the elevator incident, perhaps when Blasey Ford sees her house with its strange-looking two front doors she might think not of her assailants and her trauma, but of Archila and Gallagher, whose momentary power held open the doors of privilege for all to see. Political action is a tonic for those who feel powerless. "This is a demonstration that what thousands of people have been doing—telling our stories and standing up for ourselves—is working," Archila said afterward.

Courage is contagious, and, as all those who watch HGTV know, renovation can be habit-forming. You might plan to start with the House, and before you know it you are taking on the Senate. Where will it end? HGTV's ubiquitous "open concept" is what we, in democracies, call *transparency.* How far should we go to achieve it? Just move a few walls? Take it down to the studs? Or demo the whole thing entirely and start over? Whatever we do, it will take courage. We are lucky to have these several reminders of what that all-too-rare virtue looks like in action; especially because we know that old house will not just yield to our plans. It will fight hard to defend itself. It has termites and rot, and it is built in a swamp, but it will resist renovation, down to the last (would-be) stud. That is why we need to recall the calm and the clamor of all the protesting women who, in the fall of 2019, came to the Capitol.[2]

14

No Collision

Opting Out of Catastrophe

On his way to the G20 summit in Buenos Aires in the fall of 2018, President Trump was asked about a key finding of his own administration's dire climate report, which warns that climate change will cost the U.S. economy hundreds of billions of dollars, possibly up to 10 percent of GDP by the year 2100.[1] Trump replied, "I don't believe it." Eighteen months later, he would go on to say more or less the same about the coronavirus and the health professionals' predictions it would spread.

"I don't believe it." These four words typify the president's penchant for opting out of common sense and consensus, rejecting research and facts, preferring instead to go with his own brain, gut, or even genes. (He says he understands science because his uncle, John Trump, was a scientist—on MIT's faculty for decades.[2]) And, sure enough, the United States got its own clause in a G20 statement, refusing again to join the signatories of the Paris Climate Agreement in a commitment to tackle climate change.

The same four words—"I don't believe it"—echo those of a character, John, in Lars von Trier's science fiction art film *Melancholia* (2011).[3] In the film, a family at a remote country estate deals in various ways with disturbing news: there are widespread predictions of an imminent collision between Earth and a rogue planet. John, the paterfamilias, rejects them all. Strange animal behaviors and other portents suggest the catastrophists are right, but John sees the forecasters as mere showboats. "Prophets of doom," he calls them. Worse yet, fake news: "They'll write whatever they can to attract attention." Invoking his own preferred scientists, John forecasts a near miss. Looking up at the sky through his own very large telescope, John reassures his panicked wife and anxious son that the dire predictions they hear about on the news are belied by what he can see with his own eyes. Don't look at the Internet, von Trier's John tells his wife. Trust me. Who you gonna believe? The fake news? Or me? Tracking the rogue planet's movement, John says again and again that there will be no collision, as if repeating it will make it true.

Wealthy, with a remote estate sporting a private road and its own golf course, John has all the confidence of a man insulated from harms that affect the rest of us. His habituation to private privilege is evident when his butler, an older man named Little Father, cleans up John's messes only moments after he makes them. Unsurprisingly, then, when John realizes he has erred in his calculations, he seeks out a private escape: he takes the sleeping pills his wife has been saving for their son and abandons his family, leaving them on their own to face the implacable certainty of world destruction.

The Johns of the world today, many of whom have benefitted from the work or largesse of their own little fathers, surely have ample supplies of sleeping pills to be used in the event of catastrophe. But they are also turning to other escapes. Over the last few years several Silicon Valley entre- preneurs have bought multimillion-dollar doomsday bun- kers from a Texas company for use in New Zealand. (The company's slogan: "We don't sell fear. We sell preparedness," as if possessed of an Occam's razor to divide them neatly.[4]) "At the first sign of an apocalypse," reports Bloomberg News, "the Californians plan to hop on a private jet and hunker down." Said former prime minister of New Zealand John Key, "There comes a point at which, when you have so much money, allocating a very tiny amount of that for 'Plan B' is not as crazy as it sounds."[5]

Who doesn't want a Plan B? Asylum seekers and climate refugees certainly do, and they act accordingly when they take to the road seeking refuge elsewhere. Millennials do, too, according to the *New York Times*, which reports rather breathlessly on those who are buying land in the Catskills, Oregon, and Vermont—places in the U.S. least likely to experience extreme weather in the coming years: "They are following in the footsteps of billionaires like Peter Thiel, who is investing in real estate in New Zealand in case a cli- mate apocalypse occurs."[6]

The New Zealand Plan B is not for caravans from the south or for the kind of millennials who head north; it is for Gulfstreamers and one-percenters, wealth-migrants such as Thiel with money enough to buy New Zealand citizenship, land, private jets, and a Texas-made bunker or two. In a world of opt-outs, however, nobody's edge is permanent, not even that of the super-rich. One day, some of today's wealth- migrants may be stunned to learn that New Zealand is just a poor man's Mars.

The presidency comes with a Plan B of its own (though Trump, who has called the White House "a real dump," may find it wanting[7]). According to Elaine Scarry's *Thinking in an Emergency* (2011), there are several presidential bunkers, and one lies in the mountains of Virginia: "a man-made cavern large enough to contain three-story buildings and a lake—'a lake' [that is], one journalist observed, 'large enough for water-skiing.'"[8]

But aside from the presidential Plan B, the United States does little else to prepare for emergencies. We have phone alerts and emergency broadcast signals, earthquake and fire drills in schools, but there are no detailed state or federal government plans that we all know of for orderly evacuation, mass emergency hospitalizations, or shelter provision. When in January 2018 residents of Hawaii received mistaken phone alerts stating that there was an incoming ballistic missile threat, residents were advised simply to "seek immediate shelter." Where?

By contrast, Scarry points to certain communities in the Canadian province of Saskatchewan, which hold regular emergency drills and reviews of billeting and supplies to prepare everyone for emergencies. That way when the fire comes or a flood occurs, everyone will know what tool to bring and where to meet to coordinate action. But these preparations do still more than that: they also keep people thinking and acting like a public, with shared concerns, responsibilities, and attachments to public things and common purposes. The lack of emergency infrastructure in the United States leaves us on our own, to fend for ourselves. The majority of Americans may not be climate change deniers, but we live as if we are in denial, as if all of us, not just the current president, "don't believe it."

Writing in 2011, and focused on nuclear rather than climate catastrophe, Scarry contrasts the United States to Switzerland, which "has enough shelter space (including home dwellings, institutions, hospitals, and public shelters) for 114 percent of its population."[9] The U.S. has no such plan. Scarry warns that if (when?) the time comes for the United States to move the president outside D.C. to a presidential bunker, those left out of the calculation may surprise government elites by refusing to comply with directions. Privileged evacuees will have badges or uniforms that mean they must be let through to the front of a line, to get on a bus, pass through a traffic jam, or board a helicopter. But will the crowds part peacefully for them in the name of the public good? Unhabituated to being a "public," attached not to the common good but to calculations of personal advantage, what will they do? Who knows? On that day, the opt-out's dependence on popular acquiescence, or subjugation, will be starkly clear.

Scarry imagines recalcitrant crowds, but, to her credit, she does not consider the possibility that political leaders might simply use violence to clear the way. Silicon Valley's getaway artists do not fail to consider that possibility. Bloomberg reports that a prominent venture capitalist "has in his garage a bag of guns hanging from the handlebars of a motorcycle. The bike will allow him to weave through traffic on the way to his private plane, and the guns are for defense against encroaching zombies that may threaten his getaway." "Encroaching zombies"? Is that a pet term for neighbors and fellow citizens?[10]

There are other Plan Bs, too. They may be less exclusive than those reserved for political and economic elites, but they remain problematic—not because they opt out of the public, but because of what they propose we opt into. For example, scientists are currently working on new solar radiation management methods that promise to re-cool the earth and manage climate. Such techniques seem drawn from dystopian fiction designed to teach the tragic lessons of hubris. Should we "spray sea water up out of the oceans to seed clouds and create more 'whiteness'" in order "to reflect the heat of the sun"? Or should we "put mirrors in space, carefully located at the point between the sun and the Earth where gravity forces balance" and thus reflect up to "2 percent of the sun's rays harmlessly into space"?[11] Audre Lorde once warned against such techno-utopianism. "Sometimes we drug ourselves with dreams of new ideas. The head will save us. The brain alone will set us free. But there are no new ideas . . . to save us," Lorde said, "only old and forgotten ones," and it will take "renewed courage to try them out."[12]

As many commentators have noted, it seems easier these days for people to imagine blotting out the sun than to imagine the end of capitalism—the growth-addicted economy that got us here and to which we seem tethered to the bitter end. Ending capitalism, or at least moderating it, would require courageous moral and political leadership, from above and below. Instead, we follow scientists whose hollow assurances that they can blot out the sun recall Melville's Ahab in one of his madder moments: "Talk not to me of blasphemy, man; I'd strike the sun if it insulted me."[13]

Sparring with the sun may well be the next stage of the slow violence of climate change. "It's going to be a slow, gradual burn, if you will," said Vivek Shandas, founder of the Sustaining Urban Places Research Lab, to the *Times*.[14] New technologies may buy us more time, as the solar radiation managers promise. But the very idea of "buying time" evokes the Plan B logic of opt-outs and buy-ins that betray the democratic idea of public things. The Democrats' current proposal of a Green New Deal, by contrast, invites us to think and act like a public invested in and by a public thing—climate health, yes, but also equality, American ingenuity.

"This is going to be the New Deal, the Great Society, the moon shot, the civil-rights movement of our generation," said then-incoming congresswoman Alexandria Ocasio-Cortez at a town hall event. The Green New Deal invites us to move away from transactional calculation and zero-sum games. It dares to dream, and dream big. Writing in the *Atlantic*, Robinson Meyer says that the Green New Deal is a slogan "like 'Medicare for All' or 'Free Community College' or 'Abolish ICE,'" but, like the best slogans, it is also "a worldview, a promise, and a vision of how life would be different after their passage."[15] We could add to this list a current and suddenly widely known (as of June 2020) American political slogan: Defund the police, which is a dream too—about a society where life matters.[16]

In the 2020 emergency of Covid-19, money was found early on by the federal government to stop the (economic) bleeding of a sudden shutdown. True, the distribution of funds was inequitable and, for many, inadequate and the much-needed follow up to it never came. Still, we now know that it is possible to respond to an emergency with trillions of dollars and not just with the hope-dashing question "But how will we *pay* for that?" What remains open to question is whether we can mobilize *as a public* to work together to prevent emergencies and plan for them, rather than just try and staunch the bleeding after they hit. The public constituted by the virus in 2020, like the one that will face climate catastrophe, is not unified and equal. Different regions, races, and classes endure asymmetric exposure, have unequal access to remediation, and suffer asymmetrically. Persons of color die at much higher rates from the virus than whites do. What this means is that emergencies do not make publics. Not even a public health crisis can do that. They solicit us into a public, but we need to accept the invitation: this means it is up to us whether we decide to be burden-sharing, mutuality-supporting members of a shared and common thing or to seek out our individual or tribal advantage. The latter options involve blaming those who are vulnerable for their vulnerability, as when we talk of preexisting conditions. Such talk indemnifies the inegalitarian structures that cause diabetes and other comorbidities and allows them to land especially hard on some communities and not others.

In *Melancholia*, the end of the world comes out of nowhere. The disaster imagined by the film is not one we have anticipated—nuclear war, climate catastrophe, viral contagion—but the seemingly random end of everything. It is a perversely fitting end: a rogue planet bucking the (solar) system destroys a world of rogue individuals who take pride in doing the same.[17] We may not get the emergency we expect, the film suggests, but rather the emergency we deserve.

As for those north-bound millennials who would opt out of collectivity and seek isolation and control, Bruce Riordan of the Climate Readiness Institute has some advice: "Sure, you can grow your own vegetables, but what about wheat and grains? And what happens when you need medical attention?"[18] Shandas, too, underlines the importance of mutual dependence: "Pulling away and isolating yourself is one of the most dangerous things you can do." Joining up with others actually provides the power that opt-out individualism promises but cannot deliver. Old (so-called) democratic ideas about equality, mutuality, the power of action in concert, public things, and a shared mission are sometimes dismissed as cumbersome by climate experts who say we need change fast; but they may be the kind of old ideas that—combined with courage—will light the way.

Our need for these old ideas was illustrated rather starkly, just a year after this essay was first published, by anti-maskers in the U.S. who, during the coronavirus outbreak, demand the right to enter stores or malls without masks. They want to opt out of the federal CDC health guidelines as if they could opt out of the disease itself. The president encouraged them, openly and obliquely. The disease is not coming for them, he suggested, when he spoke of good bloodlines at a Ford factory in Michigan (as he violated state rules by appearing there without a mask). Most commentators rightly heard the dog whistle of racism in the word "bloodlines," part of Trump's off-script praise for Ford Motor Company's founder, Henry Ford, a famous anti-Semite who inspired Hitler. But in the context of the pandemic there was another dog whistle blown that day: those with good bloodlines don't need to wear masks. Until that point, anyway, in May 2020, the hardest hit by the virus were the old, the infirm, the health-compromised, the brown and the Black, all the kinds of people on Hitler's to do list before, during, and after his genocide of European Jewry. When Trump did later catch the virus, he seemed to claim the cure was worth the disease. He left the hospital crowing that he felt "twenty years younger."

Melancholia ends with John's wife, son, and sister-in-law sitting inside a bare tepee, through which the impending catastrophe sounds. In his absence, the three hold hands. That may not be consolation. But it may be instruction. Choosing to face the end together, they reject the opt-out for the sake of solidarity, move from patriarchy to a new kind of kinship, and determine to face reality together rather than escape it alone.

15

Epstein, Barr, and the Virus of Civic Fatigue (with Sara Rushing)

I don't know if we can laugh at a virus yet, not so soon after the recent horrors of the Covid-19 coronavirus. But if we can, the one to laugh at would be the one that ravaged the 1980s and with which many still live now: it is called "Epstein-Barr" and is related to what is more commonly known as "mono."

Uncannily, the old "Epstein-Barr" virus, in the news in the 1980s, maps onto the names of Jeffrey Epstein and William Barr, both in the news in the summer of 2019. Epstein—arrested finally on credible charges of child trafficking and rape—died in custody where his safety was the responsibility of William Barr's Justice Dept. They say it was suicide. The coincidence of the two men's names and that of the old virus led me and Sara Rushing to join forces to explore the current illness of American politics as a variation on the original Epstein-Barr syndrome, as if it had mutated, as viruses do, from a physical to a political auto-immune disease.[1]

In 1964, British scientists discovered the first virus known to directly cause cancer in humans. The virus is a nearly universal "preexisting condition," affecting 90 percent of the world's adult population. In the industrialized West it rarely causes cancer, appearing more commonly as mononucleosis, which causes exhaustion, sore throat, stiffness, pain, and fever. In healthy bodies, people carry the virus but typically don't get sick. In weak bodies, whether personal or political, the effects can be devastating and recurrent.

At the Simply Health website, the Epstein-Barr Virus (EBV) is said to "often lie dormant." It might be hidden for years in New York City mansions, Florida golf resorts, or offshore islands, for example. But "when your immune system weakens, whether it is because of stress, or another illness," or the Republican Party, "the EBV can break free and multiply," and suddenly it seems to be everywhere, operating out in the open, maybe even right next door.

"Given how common the infection is, it's better to have a good understanding of the symptoms . . . to protect yourself and keep everything under control. As you [or your democracy] age and your immune system gets weaker, the possibility of an EBV outbreak increases." The website doesn't give a specific age but 250 years old, give or take, seems about right.

The problem is, diagnosis is difficult, since "EBV causes many symptoms that are commonly shared with other illnesses." For example, what looks like voter apathy may turn out to be gerrymandering. What look like free markets may turn out to be oligarchical power structures. What looks like sex with underage women might turn out to be child rape. And what look like concentration camps on your border . . . might turn out to be concentration camps on your border.

Simply Health makes clear that "prolonged fatigue is one of the most common symptoms of EBV reactivation. . . . If you feel like you have been leading a rather healthy lifestyle with a selective diet, but you just feel tired and low energy all the time for no apparent reason," or because you are

constantly watching the news, checking Twitter, going to marches, donating to candidates, texting to mobilize voters, doing public writing, while still trying to live your life, raise your kids, and do your job, then . . . Simply Health advises helpfully, "it's time to look into the root cause of the problem."

Worryingly, many Americans will recognize the symptoms: "You will not be able to function properly when it hits you, because of the low energy level you have. You may try different medication," if you can afford one, "but nothing seems to work. If you have gone to the doctor, and he still doesn't know the real cause of the issue, ask him about the possibility of an EBV test" (but first, ask if your insurance will cover the test). Could it be Epstein-Barr?

Epstein-Barr may cause the sore throat that Simply Health lists as the next symptom. Yes, it's hard to swallow. It may be from mono, but perhaps it's from yelling at the news as it flies out of your TV, radio, or laptop assaulting you with the latest obscenities. The sore throat, says Simply Health, is a sign "that your immune system is being attacked." The antibodies that once protected you from the virus are no longer up to the task: judicial institutions, the rule of law, Congress, most of the watchdog media, and others that you normally count on to preserve your system's health have let the virus reactivate, and now you are its unwitting host.

Simply Health instructs those infected to "avoid crowded places" so as not to spread contagion, and in the age of Covid-19 that goes double. But we need to find new ways to crowd together instead, in the hope of infecting others with a different, healthy contagion, our contagious horror at what is happening and contagious enthusiasm for what we could achieve together were we to find our common ground. You'll want to take to your bed, yes. But that feeling in your stomach is telling you not to. Listen to it.

Simply Health suggests that "if you work or live in a stressful environment, try to find ways to change it so you can live stress-free." Analgesics and anti-depressants will only get you so far. You will need to address the enabling conditions that let the virus reactivate and flourish. Real change is the only solution.

While we do the hard work of (re)democratizing the U.S., maybe we can also entertain ourselves by naming more diseases after *all* the wrongdoers. Here is one: acostitis—a strange syndrome in which, though you are burning with fever, no thermometer can record your temperature. Early detection is especially key for this one, but a 10+ year lag is often suffered by patients (by which we mean victims). Or McConnellopathy, also known as swamp-foot, known for attacking the brain by way of the neck. Or there is also Collinitis, an inflammation of the digestive system that comes with disappointment, but no amount of head-shaking and sighing can cure it.

It is said that laughter is the best medicine, but really laughter is most effective when taken with a large dose of collective action. So ask your doctor if democracy might be right for you.

The civic fatigue that Sara Rushing and I jokingly dubbed "Epstein-Barr Syndrome" aims to put voters back in their place, to keep them at home, dispirited, and on the sidelines. In the December 2019 British election, false Facebook pages did the work: they spread cynicism ("they're all liars") aiming "to drive down turnout and up support for the 'strong man' who wasn't promising too much, but who pledged to get politics out of your face rather than using it to improve your life"; or empower your class or neighborhood.[2] The question for us is how to respond to that kind of depoliticizing PTSD (Post-Traumatic Stress Disorder) and open the way to a new one: let's call it a Politics That Sustains Democracy? (It is to be hoped that it was the start of such a long-term politics when Americans voting in the 2020 presidential election in the U.S., with the largest turnout ever, elected Joe Biden and Kamala Harris.)

16

Mueller, They Wrote

Commenting on the televised Mueller testimony, James Poniewozik, of the *New York Times*, noted the difficulty of adapting big books for the small screen. "Asked to Put On a Show, Mueller Wishes You'd Read the Book," was the witty headline. But what happened on July 24, 2019, was more like an episode of live reality TV.[1]

The thing about live reality TV is that it doesn't always go the way you expect. Regular TV programming, reality TV included, is scripted and edited. Only on live television might something actually *happen*. Janet Jackson's "costume malfunction" at the Super Bowl halftime show years ago is an example. When something happens on television, a malfunction, or possibly dysfunction, the surprise actually verifies the "reality," the liveness, the humanness of the show.

Yesterday, something happened.

The big surprise was that the giant who terrified Trump so much that he tried at least twice to have him fired (and then tried to cover that up, asking White House Counsel to lie about it) is not so gigantic after all. Mueller is nearly seventy-five years old, and he is not a reality TV star but a measured lawyer and bureaucrat who may be a bit hard of hearing and whose speech and comprehension are a bit slowed, perhaps by age, perhaps by temperament.

What should have terrified Trump, and probably did, was not Mueller, as such, but what his name stands for: the cadre of mid-career lawyers hired by Mueller to do the work of the investigation Mueller was charged with running. They were not on hand to testify, they were not allowed to be called, but they should have been called in to testify. Indeed, we learned from the hearings how important their testimony could be, and we learned why William Barr's DOJ was so keen to prevent it.

Investigations, just like governments and social movements, are not the work of single men but of networks of diverse people working together, sometimes in concert, sometimes at odds, to make things happen. Those who say, "I alone can fix it," or who believe it when someone says that, are not only foolish. They also diminish the unique kind of power that is generated only by institutions, collectivities, or partnerships. Anyone who has ever played or worked on a team, marched in a protest, or celebrated an electoral victory knows the sheer joy of being together with others in power. The people of Puerto Rico were surely experiencing that at the same moment as Mueller testified, as they drove one corrupt leader after another from office that same summer.

In yesterday's hearing there was a small but important example of the power of more-than-one. Adam Schiff and Robert Mueller seemed to have a kind of mind-meld when Schiff asked a series of pointed, short questions that assessed the moral and political implications of the report's finding.

SCHIFF: . . . From your testimony today, I'd gather
    that knowingly accepting assistance from a foreign
    government during a presidential campaign is an
    unethical thing to do.
MUELLER: And a crime in certain circumstances.
SCHIFF: To the degree that it undermines our democ-
    racy and our institutions, we can agree that it's
    also unpatriotic.
MUELLER: True.
SCHIFF: And wrong.
    . . .
We should hold our elected officials to a higher stan-
    dard than mere evidence of criminality.
MUELLER: Absolutely.
SCHIFF: You've held yourself to a standard of doing
    what's right.
MUELLER: I would hope.
SCHIFF: [You] have.[2]

So clear and concerted was this back and forth that it
offered a compelling counter to the lone actor myth that
continues to bewitch American politics. As often happens in
circumstances of cooperation and collaboration, Mueller

became more himself, not less so, as he entered into this dialogue with Schiff.

As the political theorist Hannah Arendt notes, action in concert generates power; it does not consume it. It is, as we might say today, the greenest kind of power there is. But just as green power requires storage devices like batteries to preserve it, so too action in concert requires storage devices of its own. Like wind and sun, events come and go and take their energy with them. Stories are the storage devices that store the power of the event so we can draw on it later. When we tell the story well, we may keep the energy going longer. A story that energizes is a better storage battery.

Some are already at work, harnessing the energy of yesterday's event not to batteries but to energy depletion machines. Republicans have declared victory because, they say, Democrats did not get the TV moment they supposedly wanted (no "J'accuse!" from Mueller). But that is what Republicans do—they declare victory. Remember "Mission Accomplished," George Bush's declaration of victory in Iraq on May 1, 2003, a mere six weeks into the American military involvement in Iraq that went on for almost a decade (some say it is ongoing). The tactic is also Trump's. This what he does, even if in so doing he defies reality. He will declare victory at his sentencing hearing one day (God willing).

We need to take our bearings not from these depletion machines of dissemblance but from the human moments in yesterday's hearings. Mueller's poignant vulnerability is one such moment. Another was provided by two of his departures from the expected script.

He had made clear he would volunteer nothing and certainly say nothing new. And yet he did so twice (maybe more). In response to Schiff, Mueller agreed that "knowingly accepting assistance from a foreign government during a presidential campaign is [not only] an unethical thing to do," as Schiff put it; it is also, Mueller *added,* "a crime." Certainly "a crime in certain circumstances."

The second departure, as *Vox* reported, "one of the few times . . . Mueller actually interjected and elaborated in response to a question," was to tell the House Judiciary Committee "he made hiring decisions based on 'the capability of the individual to do the job' and to do it 'seriously and with integrity.'"[3] What *Vox* does not note is that Mueller actually strung out the word "integrity" in that moment so that what we heard was something more like "in-teg-ri-ty." Every letter was articulated by Mueller, whose delivery was slowed not by age but by moral seriousness.

To this our only response as storytellers of the event must surely be R-E-S-P-E-C-T. We express that respect by telling the story of what happened yesterday in ways that preserve and harness the energy of the event, to nourish those fighting to (re)democratize American institutions, and to ground our efforts in history.

17

Unbelievable

Scenes from a Structure

Watching the new Netflix series *Unbelievable* has made me remember some things I'd forgotten.

I now recall when I first heard the word "manipulative." It is a word I—and my parents, who were not fluent English speakers—learned from my older brother and sister, who accused my mother of being manipulative. She was. I am sure I just overheard it that first time in some conversation that did not include me, since I was the youngest by far in the family. I recall that first hearing of the word because it gave me pleasure to finally have a word to name what was going on in our house. I recall, too, my father's bemused expression upon hearing that word—"manipulative." His expression conveyed an awareness that this was a new word, a BIG word. He nodded as he took it in. His bemusement let his children know they would not succeed in besting him with new fancy words in English. Nice try. There was no acknowledgment from him that a new word might be needed *because* all the old ones had failed.

For my part, I am often delighted by new words. Take "gaslighting," for example. What an efficient word. I LOVED learning it! But it arrived late; I was already in my thirties. If I had had it earlier, it would have saved me some time. I recall an argument with my mother when I was in my late teens. She was looking me straight in the eye and lying to me about something, over and over. I lost it. I remember pointing to her dark brown wood kitchen cupboards and saying (maybe I was screaming), "Do you want to know how to drive someone crazy? Tell them every day these cupboards are white. Point to their dark brown doors, and then say without hesitation: 'these cupboards are white.' Eventually, the person will lose their mind." I recall going on like this for several minutes. If only I had known the word "gaslighting," I could have been more efficient not only in communicating my distress but in understanding it.

She wasn't *trying* to make me lose my mind. It is just that other things were more important to her. I knew that. *Lots* of things were more important than me. What men thought was more important than me. What people might say was more important than me. Money was more important than me. Status was more important than me. Getting me married was more important than me. Mostly I fought all that. But sometimes I gave in. When I came home from graduate school for visits, she would often have a "match" waiting for me, a date—the son of friends; good people with standing in the community or in some other community. They were always "fine people," and he was always a "fine boy." I almost always refused. One time I went. He seemed nice. He was a doctor; a draw for her, not for me. He took me to a club and got me a drink. I became terribly dizzy; I was embarrassed to be sick and said I had to go to the bathroom. I asked someone where it was. The room was spinning. I spent what felt like an hour frantically wandering around the small club trying to get to it. No matter which way I turned I seemed to end up back in the same place. I blacked out. When I opened my eyes, I was right in front of the Ladies. A miracle. I went in and sat down with my head between my knees and tried to feel better. In a while the worst of it passed.

I went back out and found my date. What took you so long? he asked. I said I had to leave because I was ill. I remember he looked irritated. He said I must have drunk too much, but I didn't think so. I remember feeling confused by his response. He said he would take me home, but when we were in his car, he suggested we go to his place, where he did not rape me. That does not make him a hero, because he tried.

Had I told my mother what happened, she would not have believed me. She almost certainly would have suggested I must have misunderstood his intentions. And she definitely would have told me I should never have gone to his apartment. Last but not least, she would have told me not to tell anyone. For "your" sake, she would have said, and she might have believed it.

I went to see the doctor the next week to figure out what had happened to me that night in the club. He could not say, but he did say I had intuitively done the right thing. When you have an unwell stomach, all the blood rushes to your stomach from your head. That is why you feel dizzy. When you bend over and lower your head to your knees, he said, you force the blood back to your head and out of your stomach, and that makes the dizziness pass. I was inexplicably proud to have done well, but I was still mystified about what had happened. It was not until thirty years later that my memory of all this came back. I was talking about the Bill Cosby case with my own kids, telling them to be careful about what they drink, how much, and who they are with, especially because of the circulation of "these new things called roofies," I said, and right then it suddenly dawned on me: "Wait a minute, I think *I* was roofied!"

Come to think of it, that was a new word, too.

Unbelievable tells the true story of a rapist who tortures women; the just plain crappy male detectives who manipulate and gaslight one of his first victims, a troubled teenager named Marie, into retracting her claim that she was raped; and the two women detectives (modern female gothic heroines with great forensic powers!) who would have believed her but who get the case only much later, after the rapist has damaged many more lives. The series, which is rich and mesmerizing, features a cast of finely drawn characters and interweaves two parallel narratives: the story of Marie, betrayed by the male cops who don't believe her, and the story of the two women detectives who team up and work together to hunt down the rapist, following clues, collaborating together. The two pairs of detectives are powerfully contrasted. The male detectives are coasting, the women are overachieving hard workers, competent, dedicated, and professional. The men carelessly violate the victim; the women compassionately and carefully help those they work with to regain a sense of control. The process of restoration involves careful information-sharing, deference to the victim's preferences, and respect. When the facts finally come to light—Marie was telling the truth!—one of the male detectives, Parker, wonders aloud how he could have got it so wrong. He asks himself whether *he* might be one of the bad apples on the police force that he always complains about.[1] You can see the progress in his rumination . . . and also the laziness that will allow it to float away. That is how brilliant this series is.

A lovely review in the *Atlantic*, by Sophie Gilbert, sees it differently. Titled "*Unbelievable* Is TV's Most Humane

Show," the review finds hope in the moment when the "show reveals, in lingering detail, the look on Detective Parker's face as he realizes the appalling ways he mistreated a vulnerable teenager."[2] But Parker's face and comportment in that episode show something else: all the wind has been taken out of him. He sags. The two powerful women who skipped no steps and left no stone unturned have solved the case through sheer brilliance and dogged persistence. If their rows upon rows of paper piles, Post-it notes, photographs, and files, all documenting false and good leads, are the signs of excellent police work, and they are, and he says so, then he has never come close to that. And he knows it.

"*That's good work,*" Parker says, "*very good work. Looks like you have enough to send him away for a long time.*" Nope, says Rasmussen, the more senior of the two women. "*I don't count my chickens. I've seen rapists get probation too many times to count on anything.*" He nods, once again caught in the act of underachievement. What the camera sees when it lingers on him is not a predetermination of his own personal improvement but the sad dawning sense of his ineffectiveness and the pathos of what it will be like to live with the undeniable knowledge of his own mediocrity:

to know that he got it so wrong, that he has been so out-
performed, and by two women. . . . How will he live with
that?

On the steps outside, we get a glimpse of how. As he
leaves the station, accompanied by Rasmussen, Parker stops
and says:

> "*I feel like. . . um . . . I should explain. The problem is,
> uh . . . I've got nothin'.*"

Rasmussen stays silent. Somehow, she doesn't help
him with his feelings or say anything to make him
feel better. (I love her.)

He sighs. "*You know you hear about bad cops . . . guys
who make bad calls or end up hurting the people
they're supposed to protect, and I always think, like,
who the hell let him on the force, right? Just get rid of
him. . . . Maybe we should get rid of me. . . .*"

Again, silence from Rasmussen. (I could not love her
more right now.)

Parker, in the void: "*Well, thank you.*"

Rasmussen: "*You bet.*"

End of scene.

In the final episode, we see Parker has not changed at all.
It is still, incredibly, all about him. He comes to tell Marie that
her rapist has been caught and that he now understands he
was wrong to disbelieve her. But he is still uninformed about
her needs, and he puts his own needs first. He approaches her
at work, where she is alone cleaning up. She is triggered.

> "*You got a couple of minutes?*" he asks.

She breathes heavily.

Parker: "*I am sorry to bother you at work, this won't take long. Um I got some information . . . recently that I need to share with you*

. . .

a rapist was apprehended and they found eight pictures of you taken during an assault, during your assault; the one I didn't believe, the one I made you say never happened.

I figured you wouldn't want to see me but I felt (BUT **I* FELT?*)

I felt it was important to tell you in person

To look you in the eye and tell you I was wrong"

. . . and now . . . it clearly is all about him:

"*I mean I've been trying to figure out how I could have been so off.*

I wish I had an answer. I don't

I'd do anything to go back . . . and to just start all over and do right by you. I really would."

Marie: "*Well you can't.*"

Parker does later apologize (the *Atlantic* calls it "genuine"; but that is misleading . . .). It happens when Marie later comes to the station, surprising Parker at *his* workplace. She demands that apology, and he says he is "sorry; very very sorry." But his partner, who also wronged her and is standing right there, does not say anything, and when Marie leaves, with the words, "next time do better," Parker nods, but then looks around, a bit lost, at his partner, at the ceiling, at the stairwell where he stands. All that looking tells us all we need to know: he is simply not up to the task.

Hence my surprise to read in the *Atlantic* that the series' message is that we can do better. "It's possible to investigate rape cases in ways that make it more likely for victims to get justice, not less. 'Next time,' Marie tells Detective Parker, 'do better.' The great hope the series offers is that he actually might." I see absolutely no sign that he will. And many signs that he won't. In fact, given the chance, again and again, he doesn't.

The *Atlantic*'s Gilbert is not wrong that the series is both humane and hopeful. The suggestion of the series is that a better understanding of trauma would improve things for women pursuing justice, as would an understanding of rape as a crime like any other, as would more hardworking women detectives and fewer lazy male ones, and better communication all around. I am sure all that is true. But if I quibble with Gilbert and the series, it is because unbelievability is also a structure. If Parker is a little lazy, that is not just a personal flaw. His shoddy work has for many years passed muster. Why? Because the world is his oyster. The possibly radical message of *Unbelievable* is that that *world* needs to come to an end. At the same time, the series makes it quite clear that Parker will continue to be Parker. All the Parkers will.

W. E. B. Du Bois marked the work of the nefarious color line with the question, "How does it feel to be a problem?"[3] I think misogyny can be summed up by a question, too: "How does it feel to be unbelievable?" It feels like hard work, I can tell you.

Just ask the twenty-five women who have accused Trump of sexual assault. Or Lisa Page, whom he has repeatedly subjected to his "virtual," simulated assaults in front of thousands, at his rallies. Or ask the women of the State Department, like Marie Yovanovitch and Fiona Hill.[4] In their testimonies during the House impeachment hearings, Yovanovitch and Hill both described trying to navigate once familiar worlds now drenched in a fog of parallel transactions, secret foreign policies, and smear campaigns. It is like whole hosts of duplicitous men were up in the attic rummaging for lost jewels while the professionals, women, were on the main floor, clinging to what they know while trying to figure out what was going on as the lights above them inexplicably waxed and waned.

As Hill said during the House impeachment hearings, reflecting on her earlier impatience with EU ambassador Gordon Sondland, who, she later learned, was involved in trying to get Ukraine to smear Joe Biden by opening an investigation into him, "I had not put my finger on that at the moment." But she now understood what she had not earlier known: he was not just being uncooperative. "He was being involved in a domestic political errand. And we were being involved in national security foreign policy. And those two things had just diverged," she said. "I had not put my finger on that at the moment, but I was irritated with him and angry with him that he wasn't fully coordinating," she went on. "And I did say to him, 'Ambassador Sondland, Gordon, I think this is all going to blow up.' And here we are."

In the series *Unbelievable*, the women detectives know what they are up against. They are not in the dark because they are *fully* in charge, not delegated, gaslighted, worked around, and betrayed. They pile up the evidence and the paperwork because they know nonetheless and full well what structure they are in, what errands it pursues, what leads it lets lapse. Their diligence is impressive, and it solves the case. They keep going, in order to make conviction certain, to take no chances. Their tenacity is the height of professionalism. That is why it puts Parker to shame. But that tenacity is also, and still, a symptom of misogyny. How does it feel to be unbelievable? It feels like *patriarchy*, a word I learned in graduate school. We will need a new word for what comes next.

18
Gothic Girls
Bombshell's *Variation on a Theme*

In female gothic romances like *Jane Eyre* and *Rebecca*, women triumph over the sensory and psychic disorientation deliberately inflicted on them by men whose intentions are unclear.[1] Gothics are true to the realities of democratic experience, where the people are not sure if their laws and institutions aim to represent or abandon them, where rather than collectivize their efforts for the public good, institutions may be isolating citizens from each other, funneling funds to private accounts for nefarious purposes, dividing us up so as better to dominate us, lying so that we come to doubt what we saw or heard.

In such a world, citizens need the detective skills of gothic heroines—close reading, following clues, listening to one's inner voice, and healthy distrust—as well as the understanding of many of them that such skills are rooted in community or fellowship. The two women detectives in *Unbelievable*, drawn from a real-world partnership that solved real-world cases, are smart and tenacious, but their partnership is everything.[2] The best gothic heroines seek out partnerships that heal the effects of isolation and self-doubt, elevate their minds, and nourish their senses and spirits for common purpose. Most are too savvy for just romance. Gothic heroines want power.[3]

Perhaps the best recent addition to the archive of female gothics in film is *Bombshell*, in which the female gothic's remote aristocratic retreat (typically a scary castle on a hill) is replaced with an office tower in downtown New York: Fox headquarters.[4] One would expect the film to open with the daylit ambience of work, since the *mise en scene* is office life. But the film opens with the camera lingering on the building in a long shot, as the narrator explains which various seats of power are located on which of the building's different floors. It is dark out. That long, dark, lingering shot is a gothic tell.

We are entered into the dark story with Kayla, a composite character based on over twenty real women, who anticipates the real-life Kayleigh who would rise to prominence in the White House just a few months later. Kayla is a young woman from a protected, conservative, Christian background who wanders into the big-city world of Fox News, where her virtue will be tested. She does not pass the test. Manipulated by secret scripts and stealthy powers, her ambition and inexperience are exploited. Her experience is not singular. She represents the early years of all the Fox women, and indeed her story is told in a braided way, along with two others at later life stages. Kayla Pospisil is in her twenties, her whole career ahead of her; Megyn Kelly, in her forties, is at the apex of hers; and Gretchen Carlson, fifty, is facing the nadir that the magic of television visits on women of a certain age.[5]

Bombshell's brilliant innovation on the gothic formula is its simultaneous focus on all three of these women, each at a different stage of life and power, trying to escape the clutches of the castle's evil ogre. The ogre is Fox's Roger Ailes, who says he has been called Jabba the Hutt, whom he does uncannily resemble with his flesh over-spilling his leather chair. He virtually licks his lips when a young woman enters his lair. Kayla, the youngest of the women, arrives to the big city full of confidence but succumbs to the ogre. In the middle, Megyn Kelly flails a bit, but she makes sure to get what she can from Ailes, who understands television and teaches her its tricks. The oldest of the women, Gretchen Carlson, sues Ailes and wins a nondisclosure-secured settlement because she is cannily well-prepared to do so. In the end, Kelly joins the Carlson lawsuit. These three women represent the three stages through which the best female gothic heroines pass: innocent vulnerability, efforts to control and profit from the situation without fundamentally altering it, and, finally, stealthy and then open rebellion that turns the tables on the ogre.[6]

Recording early on Carlson's secret meetings with her lawyers as they plot strategy, the explicit text of *Bombshell* points to the power of law to achieve some justice. But implicitly the film suggests the real power is elsewhere: in the women's potential sorority. The three women, sequestered by circumstance and riven by rivalries deliberately sown by Ailes, struggle alone, in isolation, each faced with the specific challenges of her own circumstances and life-stage in a hostile workplace setting. But, by showing them simultaneously, the film ignites viewers' imaginations: what if the women joined up to gather their power collectively against the predations of Ailes? Could they, together, have ousted him and all the other predators? What prevents that from happening?

When over twenty women sign on to Carlson's suit, it will turn out that maybe the law, which individuates, also collectivizes. But the signatories express solidarity only in ways that law invites. Their collectivity does not generate power in Hannah Arendt's sense of action in concert because the law sequences collectivity rather than mobilizing it. Moreover, law is belated: the best it can do now is to require payment of damages. Damages can open a path to a different future, but they tend to be remediative, not revolutionary. Oriented to paying for the past, not toward building a collective future, damages are for many companies just a cost of doing business. Similarly, joining a lawsuit is not usually the beginning of a new sorority. But could it be?

Not in *Bombshell*: the film's late shot of Bill Shine, newly in charge in the Fox News building after CEO Ailes has been forced out, reminds us that a fox is still in charge of the henhouse at the aptly named *Fox* News.

The film ends here, but Shine does not. In July 2018, he was named Trump's fifth communications director. Nine months later he moved to a position in the Trump reelection campaign.

19

Boxed In

Debbie Dingell vs. Donald Trump

Watching Trump at a rally in Michigan in the fall of 2019 talking about Congresswoman Debbie Dingell and her recently deceased husband, longtime congressman John Dingell, I was struck by *how* Trump spoke the words as well as by *what* he said. Commentators noted the offenses against John Dingell, the longest-serving congressman from Michigan, who died and is unable therefore to respond to the suggestion made at the rally that he may have gone to hell, not heaven. Referring to Dingell's widow, Trump said, "She called me up," to thank him for the honors bestowed on John Dingell in death, "and said it was the nicest thing and John would have been so pleased," adding that Dingell said John would be happily looking down from heaven at the ceremony. "Maybe he's looking up," Trump said, intimating that Dingell ended up in hell, instead. "I don't know. Let's assume he's looking down."

But the real target of Trump's ire that night was not the man but his widow, Debbie Dingell, who was, at that moment, in Washington, D.C., voting for his impeachment. Clearly

Trump had been harboring some wild hope that she might vote against his impeachment. In his mind, he had once done her a favor, and she owed him.

Two years earlier, when Kirsten Gillibrand sided with women accusing Trump of sexual harassment, Trump saw that as a personal betrayal, too, and he tweeted a sexual-ized accusation: "Lightweight Senator Kirsten Gillibrand, a total flunky for Chuck Schumer and someone who would come to my office 'begging' for campaign contributions not so long ago (and would do anything for them), is now in the ring fighting against Trump. Very disloyal to Bill & Crooked-USED!"[1] Used?

In the two years since, Trump has continued to, as they say, "do battle" on Twitter, no doubt imagining himself some sort of twenty-first-century gladiator. He has also led more rallies, and in the course of those he has habituated himself to sexualized impersonations that reek of the locker rooms to which calumnies like his were once confined. A mainstay of his "act" now is the simulation of sex between Peter Strzok and Lisa Page, two employees of the FBI, involved with the department's Russia investigation. He calls them "lovers" (they had an affair) and sometimes plays the role of Lisa, but mostly positions himself as Peter Strzok, breathing heavily, panting as he repeats the name Lisa.[2] (There was a plan to perform the monologue as a skit at the 2020 CPAC meeting. It was also made into a play starring Dean Cain and Kristy Swanson reading the texts shared by the two principals.)

Here is the real fantasy of the bit: the lumpy seventy-plus-year-old makes himself the fit and virile FBI agent who gets to have affairs (while, at his rallies, thousands watch!). In the bit, Trump accents the "L" in the word "lovers" and in Page's first name, his tongue lingering on his upper teeth, so that the letter itself becomes lascivious. He reenacts their "passion" with short breathy sentences that sound like something out of a bad Harlequin romance. Moving in and out of character as Strzok, Trump also positions himself as the couple's aphrodisiac, as if their concerns about his possible election are what turned them on. His obvious enjoyment of the bit is not just in its lasciviousness. He clearly also enjoys how it positions his eventual election to office as the cold shower that douses their desire. (His ē-Lection.) Even our sex belongs to him.

Had Trump been at a rally at the time of Gillibrand's #MeToo criticism of him, he almost certainly would have recalled her visit to his office in a similar way. Conveniently, her name has L's in it too.

In Michigan on December 18, 2019, Trump added to his act the story of that conversation he had with Debbie Dingell when her husband died. When he impersonated her talking to him, he used the same short breathiness he routinely uses to simulate Strzok and Page having sex. But in Michigan, the story isn't about sex, exactly, or, better, it is about what the sex is always about for Trump: domination and debt—his and the other person's respectively. When Trump uses the same breath, pace, and cadence in the Dingell story as in his retellings of his story of Strzok and Page, it is because in both a woman is being owned, claimed by a man.

> "Then you have this Dingell. Dingell. You know Dingell from Michigan, you know Dingell, you ever hear of her, Michigan? Debbie Dingell, that's a real beauty."

> (Repeating the congresswoman's name, "Dingell, Dingell," the racist from Queens here recalls a television version of his character—Archie Bunker—whose pet name for his abused wife is "Dingbat" and who

often used the phrase Trump uses here: *"that's a real beauty."*)

"So she calls me up like eight months ago. Her husband was there a long time—but I didn't give him the B treatment. I didn't give him the C or the D. I could have. . . . —I gave the A+ treatment. 'Take down the flags!' 'Why you taking them down?' 'For ex-congressman Dingell.' 'Oh OK.' 'Do this, do that, do that, Rotunda.' Everything. I gave him everything. That's OK! Don't want anything for it. I don't need anything for anything. She calls me up. It's the nicest thing that's ever happened. 'Thank you so much. John should be so thrilled. He's looking down. He'd be so thrilled. Thank you so much, sir.' I said, 'That's OK, don't worry about it.' Maybe he's looking up. I don't know. I don't know. Maybe. Maybe. But let's assume he's looking down. But I gave him A+, not A, not B+, not B. I gave him the A+, and she called me, so nice, oh. I won't go into the conversation because it's not fair to do that. But all you want to say is, let's put it this way: it was the most profuse thank-you that you could ever get. On a scale of 0 to 10, it was a 10. OK. So that was what, February or something. Now they talk about this phony impeachment. And she's out there. 'Well, we have to look seriously at our president because he may have violated the Constitution of the United States. And I can't be happy with that because I love our country. I love this and I love that.' She loves everything. I said, 'She's a no, OK.' No but I look at her and she's so sincere and what happens? 'I vote to impeach Trump.' And you know what—I didn't say—who the hell knew this was even going to come up."

"So she calls me up like eight months ago." The truth is he called her to offer condolences. And she thanked him. Did she also thank him for the honors her husband was given in death and burial? We would need a transcript to know for sure, but it seems likely the president maneuvered to be thanked, perhaps by listing all the things that were being done to honor John Dingell in death for his life's service, to which thanks would be the only polite response. Extracting the thank-you is a step in setting up the account for future repayment. In fact, although Trump said otherwise, Dingell didn't lie in state in the Rotunda before his funeral in Washington and his burial at Arlington National Cemetery. (Even if he had, control of the Rotunda belongs to the Congress, not to the president.)[3] As CNN pointed out, "Dingell did lie in state [not at the Rotunda but] at the U.S. Capitol—a massive honor, to be sure, but one conferred on him by Congress, not the president."[4]

"I gave him everything." But he didn't, actually. Congress did, and, in any case, as Debbie Dingell said the next day, her husband earned what he got through his long service. None of this matters to Trump, because he surely imagines he as president had the power to stop the congressman from getting the honors he had earned (just like Trump imagined he had the power—not the authority, but the raw power—to stop Ukraine getting the money it had been allocated, and to cut short the career of a storied U.S. diplomat, and on and on and on). He expects to be thanked for not unjustly thwarting the honors people spend a lifetime earning.

And then, absent the expected fealty from the widow, Trump simulates a sex-sounding scene of gratitude. What is the word we have for this sort of man, a man who demands to be thanked not for what he did but for what he didn't do?

For not ruining your life and everything you've worked so hard for, because he could ruin it if he wanted to? That sort of man is an abuser. He thinks, and he wants you to think, that your very existence depends on him. You must thank him for not killing you. He could do it, too.

I am reminded of the novel *Room*, in which a young woman is kept by her kidnapper for years in a tiny room that becomes her whole world, and she depends on him for everything.[5] We know of such stories in the real world, too. Sometimes the "room" is more figurative. Men like Trump often attempt to box others in, even without the kidnapping and without the room.

I want him in a "public box," Trump said about Ukraine's leader, Zelensky, as he tried to leverage the investigations he wanted. Trump's son-in-law Jared Kushner was after leverage, too, when he said in April 2020, in the middle of the Covid-19 public health emergency, that the federal stockpile of health equipment is "ours." Kushner was immediately criticized for ignorance about the federal government's role and responsibilities in relation to the states. The ventilators are the federal government's, which is supposed to manage and distribute them according to a public plan with accountability. It is a public trust, not private property. The stockpile exists so that states' needs are optimally met.

When Kushner said the ventilators are "ours," he meant that the White House would set the conditions for their distribution without accountability. The conditions were gratitude and deference. This is entirely in keeping with the Versailles mentality of the administration, in which courtiers vie for the king's favor. And the point was echoed by Trump the next day. States would, at the very least, have to ask nicely. Be nice, said Trump at around this time to Yamiche Alcindor of PBS at a White House Press briefing:

"Look, let me tell you something. Be nice. Don't be threatening."[6]

Be nice.

The public box that Trump wanted for Zelensky is not his only resort. Sometimes Trump prefers a *private* box. That was his plan with Debbie Dingell. He did her a favor, he claimed. He expected her to repay it, to be nice, and when she didn't, and when she wasn't, when she voted for his impeachment in the House, he exacted vengeance. He went to her state and mocked her.

This sort of man inserts himself into all that is otherwise causal, natural, or human so that somehow those around him are made to understand that everything they have depends on him. His will controls the air they breathe. The clothes they wear. They are all his. Or in Jared Kushner's word, "ours." Former California congresswoman Katie Hill's leaked personal photographs, posted first on conservative websites, are a man saying, "You dress and have dignity because I let you. And if I choose not to, then you lose those things." He is saying "I decide" what job you will have, what renown you enjoy. That is one reason her decision to leave Congress was so painful to so many and still rankles. It was her decision, yes; maybe: but it was driven by a man claiming power over her.

The day after Trump's Michigan rally, Debbie Dingell was asked by reporters and TV hosts if she wants Trump to apologize. No, she said, several times in response to the question. It was a smart move. Such a demand would put her into the transactional domain in which he is most comfortable and into which he has already insisted she belongs. She would be begging (for an apology), and he could be withholding, like a man in charge: You want it? Jump higher. Cook better. Change your vote.

Instead, she was photographed holding hands with Nancy Pelosi. Their clasped hands say they are not boxed in. That clasp represents the power that comes from mutuality, and it can be very powerful when wielded against the isolation that is the tyrant's tool. In this context, the American isolationism of Trump's Make America Great Again suddenly takes on a new meaning: its aspiration is to isolate all of us from friends and allies outside and next door. And, as in *Room*, it is a sick and evil aspiration.

20

Mediating Masculinity

Rambo Republicanism and the Long Iran Crisis

In January 2020, after the U.S. assassination of General Qasem Soleimani—"widely seen as the second most powerful figure in Iran"—President Trump warned Iran not to retaliate.[1] On Twitter, he said the United States would respond in turn by attacking fifty-two Iranian sites, some "at a very high level & important to Iran & the Iranian culture."[2] Others have rightly noted that the destruction of sites of cultural but not military importance is a war crime. Perhaps Trump and Eddie Gallagher, the war criminal he recently pardoned, can have a laugh about that next time they get together at Mar-a-Lago.

But why *fifty-two* sites; and what does it tell us about Trump's mindset in this self-created crisis? "Fifty-two" is a powerful number in this context. There are currently 5,200 U.S. troops in neighboring Iraq. (Responding to current events, the Iraqi parliament met in an emergency session on Sunday, January 6, 2020, and voted to expel all U.S. troops from the country.) Or perhaps the number resonates because of the B-52s that would likely deliver the threatened bombs to those fifty-two sites in Iran. As it happens, Trump did order, in a public way, a B-52 mission on January 6, 2020.[3] Of course, "fifty-two" also calls to mind a "house of cards"—there are fifty-two cards in a deck—but *house of cards* also connotes, according to Dictionary.com, a "structure or plan that is insubstantial and subject to imminent collapse," which is where we—or the White House—might be heading.[4]

Trump invited yet another interpretation of the number when he tweeted in his "WARNING" that the fifty-two targets represent the fifty-two Americans who were taken hostage in Iran in 1979 and held for over a year, after the fall of the brutal U.S.-backed Shah of Iran. But why link the 2020 assassination of Soleimani to the 1979 Iran hostage crisis? It seems to make little sense. It casts the assassination of Soleimani as retributive payback for a past wrong, even as the Trump administration tries to insist it was a proactive act of deterrence, a preventative measure aimed at stopping attacks it claimed were "imminent."

The benefit of linking now to then is that it positions Trump as Rambo, the Vietnam veteran and symbol of steroidal masculinity, played since the 1980s by Sylvester Stallone, who avenges American humiliation long after the fact. In *Rambo: First Blood Part II* (1985), the second in the multimillion-dollar film franchise, Rambo "launches a bloody rescue mission in Southeast Asia for U.S. servicemen missing in action."[5] Now, nearly four decades later, Trump says he too seeks to settle accounts.

It is no coincidence that he recently disseminated on Twitter a doctored image of himself as another of Stallone's characters, the fictional boxing hero Rocky Balboa who finally defeats his rival, Black heavyweight Apollo Creed (causing Muhammad Ali to observe that the fictional victory of the white over the Black boxer is unsurprising: "America has to have its white images"). Trump was much mocked for making himself into the rock-ribbed Rocky.[6] But it is worth noting that the desire to Stallonize himself is not merely a matter of personal vanity; it is a fundamental part of the Republican Party's cultural politics of masculinity.

Stallone insists that his Rambo character is politically neutral but "Rambo was always a product of Republican policy," Scout Tafoya noted in 2019, in a review of the most recent Rambo film, *Rambo: Last Blood*.[7] Indeed, thirty years ago, when Ronald Reagan saw *First Blood Part II* while he was in office, he joked, "Boy, after seeing 'Rambo' last night, I know what to do the next time" American hostages are taken. At the time, writing in the Christian journal *Transformation*, Jay Kesler said, "I fear the United States is on the verge of saying 'Give us Rambo!' We would rather have him than Jesus Christ. He is offering so much more of what our national psyche craves."[8] So, too, Trump is now offering the "so much more" of what "our national psyche craves."

Trump stole Reagan's electoral tag line. Make America Great Again cites Reagan's "Let's Make America Great Again," which was printed on election buttons in 1979/80.[9] And, as president, he has only praised Reagan, aligning himself with the president most admired by the Republican Party.[10] In 1987, however, while promoting *The Art of the Deal*, Trump, on the advice of conservative strategist Roger Stone, accused Reagan of being weak on the Soviet Union (two years before the Berlin Wall came down). In full-page ads in the nation's major newspapers, Trump declared, "There's nothing wrong with America's Foreign Defense Policy that a little backbone can't cure."[11]

"Fifty-two" signifies Trump's return to this old script of emasculation, first penned for him by Stone over thirty years ago. But the script is riskier now than it was then because most of the offenses for which Trump has now been impeached were likely committed then by the Reagan campaign, which got away with it. As Charlie Pierce writes in *Esquire*:

> The Reagan campaign worked covertly to keep the hostages from being released before the 1980 election. When it finally occurred, on the day that Ronald Reagan was inaugurated in 1981, we were told it was because the Iranians were afraid of the newly elected Marlboro Man in the White House, instead of the fact that sub rosa promises had been made regarding arms sales and the return of frozen Iranian assets.[12]

None of this was widely known in 1981. Much of it is still debated now (though, notably, rendering things debatable, by debating them, is a way to neutralize the power of facts). The allegations were investigated by both houses of Congress and found to lack supporting evidence. But the case was made persuasively in 1991 in a book by former U.S.

National Security Council member Gary Sick: *October Surprise: American Hostages in Iran and the Election of Ronald Reagan*, and an episode of PBS's *Frontline*.[13]

The mere mention of the number "fifty-two" all but confesses to crimes of which both Reagan and Trump have been accused (conspiring with a hostile foreign power after election, before inauguration: Iran then; Russia now). Why risk it? Because manliness is only ever as powerful as the next alpha male, and "fifty-two" is Trump's way to say he is more Rambo than Reagan. While many of us worry about who will survive this moment and how many lives will be lost in today's and tomorrow's battles of the braggarts, "fifty-two" puts the focus on a different question: Who will be the bigger man—the B-movie star or the reality TV personality?

Television is a key part of the story.[14] In 1979, ABC launched a new show specifically to cover the hostage crisis. Hosted by Ted Koppel, *The Iran Crisis: America Held Hostage* had quite a challenge to overcome, since its subject was a crisis in which, as Charlie Pierce also notes, almost nothing ever happened. Until then, such serial nonhappening was the preserve of soap operas, which depict almost nothing ever happening. But with American hostages held abroad, the nation was feminized, and so too was its newest television news show. Reporting nightly on the scene of Americans' humiliation abroad, Koppel gave up on the time of the event and adopted in its place the slow seriality of soaps, following the slowly unfolding and often sexualized politics of power abroad. The show, later renamed *Nightline*, appeared on ABC for more than thirty-five years—not quite besting the fifty-seven-year record run of the soap opera *The Guiding Light*, but certainly giving it a run for its time and money.

The televisual politics of sexualized power and the slow time of seriality are keys to Stallone's success in film, as well.

Responding to criticism, he once admitted that he is "constantly making sequels" but quipped, "Isn't a famous TV show just sequels? You watch the same damn show for ten years, but you should only make a good film once?"[15] Sequels, franchises, all are in a day's or a decade's work. With the number "fifty-two," Trump the TV personality follows Stallone's B-movie lead, hoping to serialize the eventful conflict between the United States and Iran from decades ago.

Just a couple months later, Trump would also try to take Ted Koppel's place. The nearly-midnight of Koppel's nightly show about an American crisis would become for a time, during the pandemic, the early-evening coronavirus briefing, covered by television news even though nothing ever happened. Indeed, the leitmotifs of the coverage were straight out of soap opera with that genre's characteristic twists of Versailles. Who is in and who is out of favor? Will Dr. Fauci be there? Will Dr. Birx speak up? Tune in and see! As the *Washington Post* put it, Trump "governs as if producing and starring in a reality television show, with each day a new episode and each news cycle his own creation, a successive installment to be conquered."[16] Unfortunately, as historian Lawrence Glickman points out, the *Post* and other mainstream media outlets often cover the story in that way, too, feeding the latest news cycle with the newest feud episode, wondering out loud what will happen next, rather than establishing and sticking to their own measures and criteria of coverage.[17] One obvious yardstick ought to be: what is and isn't being done by the government to stem the fatalities in a public health crisis? What plans are being made for the fair and equitable distribution of health resources, like personal protective equipment (PPE) now, and vaccines later? Is anyone profiting off the misery?

In 1987, Reagan speculated about what to do the "next time" American citizens are taken hostage. What if that time is now? Early in January 2020, the captive audience of the U.S. was promised a spinoff when it was announced that Donald Trump Jr. and Ivanka Trump were among Republican voters' top picks for 2024.[18] Fortunately, television shows are often canceled—some in their very first season; and spinoff contracts once promised often disappear into the vapor of television's airwaves. For that to happen, though, television's citizens will need to wake up. It is 5 p.m.: do you know where your voting rights are?[19] Your polling station? Your voter I.D., if your state unconscionably requires it? Your mail-in ballot? Your local organizers can help, and, once you are talking to them, you may find they need your help, too.

21
"13 Angry Democrats"?
A Noir Reading of 12 Angry Men

When Donald Trump tweets about "13 angry (and conflicted) Democrats" in the Mueller investigation (on August 3, 2018, the number was 17, and in July 2019 it was 18), he is citing the film *12 Angry Men* in the hope of killing two birds with one (Roger) Stone.[1]

Trump's "13 angry Democrats" tweet targets not only Mueller, but also Henry Fonda, the star (and coproducer) of *12 Angry Men*, who personified gentle masculinity and liberal fairness for mass audiences in this beloved 1957 film about white prejudice and the power to overcome it. This was also Fonda's persona in several other films from the period to which MAGA calls us to return (*Young Mr. Lincoln* [1939], *Mr. Roberts* [1955], *Advise and Consent* [1962]).

Repeating "13 angry Democrats!," Trump positions him-*self* as the good guy who loudly exposes corruption and recasts the quiet strength of men like Fonda as weakness. The aim is to shift our sympathies from the avowed hero of *12 Angry Men* to the film's Trump-like villain: the most virulent white racist, Juror #10, who says, "I'm sick and tired of

facts." Juror #10 later lets loose a lengthy racist rant, which leads his fellow jurors, some themselves quite prejudiced, to turn their backs on him in a kind of ritual shunning. He is too much even for them.[2]

The shunning works. Juror #10 later yields when the majority votes to acquit the defendant on trial, an abused adolescent who appears "ethnic" in a way that could be read as Jewish, Italian, or Puerto Rican.

The message today from the White House is, "You don't need to yield to them any*more*." This, from the man who, in the 1980s, called for the death penalty for the unjustly accused Central Park 5. *He* is "sick and tired of facts," too.

Juror #10's shunning and yielding lead many critics to fault *12 Angry Men* for betraying the ideals it seems to want to promote. It's the wrong way to win, they say, given the film's expressed commitment to reasonableness, careful deliberation, and proper procedure. But this misses the film's most important point, which is precisely the insufficiency of liberal ideals alone to achieve justice. The point was made by William Connolly about the "Brooks Brothers Riot," men wearing button-down shirts and chinos bussed in by Republican operatives to stop the Florida recount in the year 2000 presidential election. That white male swarm, which was Astro-turfed by the Republican Party, telegraphed a threat of violence to the justices of the Supreme Court at the moment of their deliberations on Bush v. Gore.[3]

A similar mix of reasons, persuasion, and the threat of violence characterize jury deliberations in 12 *Angry Men*. The group begins eager to convict the nonwhite youth accused of murdering his abusive father. But Juror #8 (Fonda) raises questions about the case that the other jurors, in their prejudice, complacency, or indifference, had not considered. Pointing out that the system gave the unfortunate defendant an inept 'court-appointed' public defense lawyer who might have "resented being appointed" to a case with "no money, no glory, not even much chance of winning," and who inadequately cross-examined the witnesses, Fonda makes clear that if the public defender will not do his job, Fonda will. He challenges the prosecution's case, point by point, like a defense lawyer who really believes his client is innocent.

Some join Juror #8 to help counter the prosecution's case, which went largely unanswered in court. But not everyone appreciates his gifts: one juror mocks the others for being easily manipulated by a "golden-voiced preacher [who] starts tearin' your poor heart out about some underprivileged kid just couldn't help becomin' a murderer—and you change your vote!" (We could use many such golden-voiced preachers.)

The mocking is sometimes gendered: Some of the white male jurors dominate, others are easily bullied; one actually challenges another, saying, "What kind of a man are you?" Another calls the others "ladies" when they start to reconsider their initial, harsh judgments. Feminization is a threat.[4]

It is not just the deliberations that are in disrepair. Like much of American infrastructure now, the scene of deliberation in 12 *Angry Men* is in disrepair, too. The jury room's fan doesn't work, and so the men suffer from the heat in their closed, confined space. The clock on the wall is not working, either, and in the bathroom one of the towel machines is broken. This is the result of not just neglect but of active disinvestment: the beginning of the end of the New Deal is here in the austerity to which public things in the U.S. are subjected. No clock, no fan, no towel means you need to bring your own or do without. No committed defense attorney, just an overworked, underpaid, or uncaring public defender, means you are free to convict unjustly on the prosecution's unanswered charges or you are obliged to reason through a defense on your own. Such resort to the private is invited by all the brokenness, and it forks into these two possible paths: (1) Give up; don't bother; no one cares; or (2) Do it yourself!

We see it when Fonda goes to the adjoining men's room to wash his face and cool off. His face and hands wet, he reaches up from the sink to the towel machine next to it. He tugs on the towel, but it is stuck. He gives it a closer look to see what is wrong. He looks at the side of the machine to see if there is a lever there to override the stuck mechanism. There isn't. Still silent, he looks around the room, sees another machine, and goes to try that one. He tugs on the towel. It works. He expresses no frustration and no surprise. He dries his face and hands.

One of the jurors, a salesman, is there and chats with him, but leaves before Fonda turns to dry his face on the working towel machine. Then another juror, a laborer, walks in. Both are annoyed: Fonda is slowing down deliberations when it is obvious the accused is guilty. Fonda's towel sequence is sandwiched by these two men. The first, the salesman, had wiped his used hair comb on the working public towel that Fonda, who walks in afterward, will use for his face and hands. The second, a laborer, does not use a towel at all. He washes his face and neck with his hands, pats himself, and leaves without toweling. These are two ways of relating to public things. Treat them like garbage without worrying they are shared (the salesman and his dirty comb) or just don't use them at all (the laborer and his damp hands). They contrast with Fonda, who uses public things with care, looks to repair what he can, and does not give up on them. His patient search for levers, alternatives, and workarounds with the towel machines in the bathroom is a metaphor for his way of maneuvering around the various jurors who, like the first towel machine, are stuck and will not yield to a simple tug.

Fonda's care extends even to Juror #3, the very last racist holdout, who does finally give in to the new majority in favor of acquittal. The other jurors exit the room; Fonda stays back to attend to him and even helps him on with his jacket. (Is it an accident, though, that, as we see in this still, Juror #3's arms extend and his head hangs in a pose that recalls crucifixion? Is he Jesus or Barabbas?)

A rainstorm had saved Fonda, arriving just in time to cool the jury room and eliminate one juror's hope of getting to the ballgame that evening. There was to be no going for a walk that evening. The men return to their deliberations and agree to find the defendant not guilty. The storm ends just in time for Fonda, who has won, to walk into the bright light of a now-sunny day. The change in the weather under-writes what most critics see as the film's happy ending. They note the film's closing exchange of appreciative words between Fonda and another juror (his first supporter), after which Fonda walks off. The rain has stopped. The good guy won. The End.

But wait. What these critics do *not* note is that the film does not actually end there at all. The camera stays on the steps of the courthouse for minutes more. Then, in the back-ground, if we look closely, we can see the two most explicitly racist jurors, #3 and #10, exiting, not together but in sequence. They move fast. We don't see their faces, but their body shapes and gait are unmistakable. Their exit goes unre-marked except by the music, which turns dissonant.

At the end of the film, says one critic, Juror #10 is "irrele-vant," a "pitiful relic."[5] But, if Juror #10 is a relic, it is less in this critic's intended archaeological sense of a remnant of something long gone and more in the church's sense of retaining powers of enchantment. The film is owned in the end not by the gentle/manly Henry Fonda, dressed in white like the hero of an urban Western, but by the two rough, racist jurors and the *noir* undercurrent of pessimism, fatal-ism, and menace into which Fonda, too, is locked.

To see the film as a celebration of liberal reason requires that we ignore the film's several intimations of noir. The film uses extreme closeups that are lit and shadowed in a way that clearly references *film noir*, the genre of the locked-in. How-ever, *12 Angry Men* is not normally treated as noir. Director Sidney Lumet and his cinematographer, Boris Kaufman, are said to use the exaggerated closeups and diverse camera angles merely to liven up this mostly one-room film. But it is a noir technique to show the pores and sweat of the men's faces, suggesting they are locked in—to the jury room, by their prejudices, indeed by their very *skin* (color).

Interpreted as noir, 12 *Angry Men* shows a good man winning one battle while suggesting that goodness will not win an unwinnable war. Those two rough men will be back. Without a steady stream of Juror #8s, racism triumphs, rain or shine.[6] And that is why Trump rails ceaselessly about 13, 17, or 18 angry Democrats. Fonda's Juror #8 is his true foe, and he wants everyone else to see him that way, too. "That guy in the white suit?" we can almost hear him scoff. "You can't be serious." We had better be.

22

In the Streets a Serenade

Siena under Lockdown

Emergencies like the 2020 coronavirus public health crisis can be occasions to retrench democracy or deepen it, recommit to public things or abandon them more fully. Which will it be?

In England, in March 2020, local elections were deferred for a year as part of a more general crowd avoidance strategy designed to limit the spread of the new coronavirus.[1] England's electoral commission recommended deferring the local elections until autumn, but the government opted for a delay of one year instead, for reasons that are "not clear," an MP said. At that moment, however, West End theater performances had not been canceled, and all the seats in London's theaters were still full. Democracy may have to go on hiatus, but the show, it seems, really must go on. (Two weeks later, the theaters would close, too.)

The virus can make us go private, or it can lead us to a renewed democratic appreciation of public things, like public health services coordinated by dedicated experts working for the government and the people, data, and information gathering by a public-oriented Center for Disease Control (CDC), and contagion guidelines made public for the public, immune from political intervention.

The logical implication of the going private option includes canceling elections. If we go that way, there may be no going back.

But there is no good reason to go that way. If universities can pivot quickly to remote learning to respond to the crisis, then surely governments can figure out remote voting. We already have something like it: Absentee ballots are available in all fifty states, and of course some, like Washington State, have mail-in voting. As of May 2020, so does California, although all Trump does now is rail against it as a kind of cheating.[2]

We are now, early in the pandemic, being told to practice social distancing. It is clear from the dearth of toilet paper in the stores that many people are hoarding and have mistaken instructions to isolate and distance from others for orders to go it alone. But social isolation or social distancing is not the same thing as going private. It is, paradoxically, something we all have to do together.

Going private in an emergency means flying to your private island on your private plane with your private pilot and your private doctor. This is not social isolation. It takes the social out of social isolation and leaves only isolation.

American isolationists have long practiced the isolation without the social bit, opting out of global efforts to combat climate change; refusing the World Health Organization's timely offer of coronavirus testing kits or withdrawing from that organization altogether, as Trump would later do when he blamed WHO for the viral spread in the U.S. All these choices announce that we prefer to go it alone. We think we can beat the curve. Do better.

When disaster strikes, isolation (not the social kind) will look attractive to people used to opting out. Such people are trained to seek their comparative advantage. Opting out declares you have the power to go it on your own, that you do not need others. This to some looks like declaring independence. But such declarations of independence renounce the mutuality that underwrites the original Declaration of Independence and constitutes democratic citizenship, which announces that we are all in this together. That sense of being bound together is illustrated by the (likely apocryphal) story of the signing of the U.S. Declaration of Independence: John Hancock said that members of the Second Continental Congress, having signed the Declaration, must now "all hang together," and Benjamin Franklin replied, "Yes, we must indeed all hang together, or most assuredly we shall all hang separately."

Social isolation is social, unlike isolationism, which is antisocial. Social isolation is collaborative and neighborly. We do it by hanging together. Antisocial isolation is competitive, it seeks to survive above all else, and it wants to "win."

The social version of isolation or, as we now call it, "social distancing," led people to sing together in Italy under lockdown. The antisocial kind of isolation cannot carry a tune and may indeed be tone deaf, which means that people who go that route are deaf to the moment and will miss what it has to offer.

In Siena and other Italian cities, streets and neighborhoods have responded to the social distancing mandate by joining together in song. Their voices sound in the emptied streets. This is an example of the power of voice that, as the Italian feminist philosopher Adriana Cavarero says, is both embodied (produced by our vocal cords) and capable of traversing great distances beyond where the body is. Listening to them sing in videos posted online, one hears a yearning for mutuality in their song and evidence of its power in their common knowledge of the words and tune. When they sing in Siena, they enact citizenship's mutuality without putting each other at risk. They reach out to each other without violating the rules of contagion-prevention. I hear in their streets a serenade. If there is a show that must go on, surely it is this one: the serenade for democracy.

23
Isn't It Ironic?
Spitballing in a Pandemic

Isn't it ironic that bleach, an agent of whitening, may bring
about Trump's downfall? After everything he has done for
whiteness?

And isn't it also ironic that television, the medium that
gave life to his personal and political ambitions, may be the
instrument of his demise?

Social distancing recommends we stay six feet apart from
each other lest our speaking, sneezing, or coughing spread
viral droplets to others. Spit is a carrier of Covid-19, a danger
to public health. So is spitballing, which is what Trump
dangerously did at a White House press briefing on Thursday, April 23, 2020. Musing out loud like Jeffrey Epstein at
one of his "science" dinners, Trump asked about the powers
of disinfectants like bleach to kill the virus not only on hard
surfaces but also inside the human body. After a presenta-
tion by William Bryan, DHS acting undersecretary for science and technology, Trump said, "I see the disinfectant,
where it knocks [the virus] out in a minute—one minute—
and is there a way we can do something like that, by injection

inside, or almost a cleaning . . . so it would be interesting to check that. That, you're gonna have to use medical doctors. But it sounds interesting to me." No one objected. (Bryan, who is not a doctor or scientist, served in the army, then as a civil servant at the Defense and Energy departments, and was accused by a whistleblower of manipulating government policy to further his personal financial interests, and then lied to Congress about it.)[1]

Dr. Birx, who was there, too, and has been tasked with coordinating the federal government response to the virus, later tried to explain it all away on Fox News, and what she said rings a little bit true: "When he gets new information he likes to talk that through out loud and really have that dialogue and so that's what dialogue he's having." The issue, she implied, is not the musing: that is his process. The issue is that it happened in the wrong place at the wrong time, in front of everyone rather than behind the scenes.

But Trump knew that. He mused publicly because he hoped to give us all a peek behind the scenes. He has ideas, and his people take them seriously! See? And who knows? He himself might come up with the cure! As he said in early March, during a visit to the headquarters of the Centers for Disease Control and Prevention, "People are really surprised I understand this stuff." But they shouldn't be surprised. His uncle was, you know, a "super-genius," who "taught at MIT, like, for I think a record number of years."[2]

Digesting information live on television is good TV! Trump surely imagined that when we all watched him as he asked for more research, we would see a man in charge. But what many saw was an ignoramus setting the research agenda with his power like Jeffery Epstein did with his money. On Thursday it was like we were *all at* one of those infamous Epstein "science" dinners, listening to the great man pontificate while some of the invitees squirmed, but

stayed, perhaps thinking of the girls or the money that would come later.

In the case of Dr. Birx, I imagine more noble motivations at the start. She has spent her career fighting AIDS around the world. When Trump introduced her at one of his earlier White House coronavirus press briefings, he mentioned how committed Birx was to her work, and he also mentioned how much money the U.S. spends on that cause, singling out Africa. He said something like (I paraphrase here): *over 6 billion dollars, can you believe it—that is a lot. Maybe too much; I don't know. We'll see.* The message was clear. He put her in a box. *Your life's work? It is in my hands. . . .* So too, now, is the public's health.

Those invitees at the Epstein dinners, scientists and others from MIT and Harvard, helped whitewash Epstein, escorting him back in to polite society after he completed his very short and light prison sentence for procuring prostitution from a minor.[3] Arguably, all the president's men and women now are doing the same whitewashing work for Trump. What we saw on Thursday in the briefing room is what is going on behind the scenes: his advisors indulge Trump's bright ideas and act like they take them seriously. "I just had a thought. Look into it." At that press briefing, he did not say it like it was an order. His tone was inveigling, whispery, cajoling. He was impersonating what he imagines it looks like to have an idea. Buttressed by power with a soupçon of noblesse oblige, however, his "thought" was really a command: act like it's a good idea. Yessir, we will.

There was nothing subtle about it in this exchange with Birx:

> TRUMP: Deborah, have you ever heard of that? The heat and the light relative to certain viruses, yes, but relative to this virus?
>
> DR. DEBORAH BIRX: Not as a treatment. I mean, certainly fever is a good thing. When you have a fever, it helps your body respond. But, I've not seen heat or light as a—
>
> TRUMP: I think that's a great thing to look at. OK?[4]

OK.

The public saw exactly what Trump wanted to show us, but we interpret it differently. Where he meant to show verification—see, my staff think I'm smart!—we saw coddling; the curtain was pulled back, and we saw how, behind the scenes, this pretend-having-of-ideas is routinely treated like something worthy. Isn't it ironic that the president whose platform is built on dismissing so-called snowflakes is the most coddled man in America? His presidency is a participation trophy, and his every performance is given an A+ by his staff.[5]

Sadly, some were taken in. In Maryland, in the days immediately after the briefing, more than 100 people called emergency hotlines to ask for more information about whether disinfectant could help them against the virus. Taken aback by the criticism that followed, Trump repositioned himself.

"I'm just here to present talent. I'm here to present ideas, because we want ideas to get rid of this thing." In short, that stuff about disinfectant has nothing to do with him. His role is to host the show, like Pat Sajak, not star in it. Sometimes he might bring out Vanna White, I mean Ivanka, to help host.

Trump's televisual power has served him well, as has his determination to get free TV airtime by holding "briefings" that are really rallies. But unlike at the rallies he stopped holding for a while because of the pandemic, the press at the briefings responds to his charges and insults. Instead of his rallies' two-hour-long monologues, he is now pressed into question-and-answer exchanges that have become a bit more like debates, and his daily pummeling of the press sometimes now backfires. Unlike earlier in his term, the press seems less inclined to coddle and more inclined to, well, press. Together every day, day after day, insulted on camera ("I am the president and you are fake news," said Trump to the *Washington Post*'s Philip Bump this week), something has intensified in the White House press corps, which seems to have summoned new resources of inquisitiveness, resistance, and solidarity.

"That's not true," one reporter was heard to object when Trump claimed the press was celebrating the casualties of the virus (repeating an earlier calumny of his, that he saw American Muslims celebrating on 9/11). Another, when called on, deferred to a colleague who had been earlier cut short. And on Friday, April 24, the day after the bleach episode, there was what Jim Acosta called "almost an act of civil disobedience." White House officials tried to force Kaitlan Collins of CNN to change her assigned front-row seat to one in the back assigned to the *Washington Blade*'s Chris Johnson. Both reporters refused to switch as instructed even when threatened with action on the part of the Secret Service. The White House relented. But Trump took no questions that day. He spoke uncharacteristically briefly, and, when he left the briefing room, he performed his pique by turning on his heel the second Pence stopped speaking. That day, anyway, Trump knew how to read the room.[6]

By May 11, 2020, things would deteriorate further. CBS's Weijia Jiang asked Trump why he would tell her (an American) to go "ask China" when she asked why he seems to be competitive with other countries on the question of which has the most virus tests. Trump tried to cut her short by calling on CNN's Kaitlan Collins, but Collins invited Jiang to finish first. Then, when Collins stepped up to go next, Trump tried to skip her, in retaliation, and chose Yamiche Alcindor, but Alcindor refused and deferred to Collins, her CNN colleague, to go first, since Collins had been called on already. At that point, faced with three women collaborating (recalling Pelosi and Dingell's hand clasp of power), Trump abruptly left the briefing and took no more questions.

Trump knows how to control a news cycle. His spitballing about disinfectant distracted attention from the whistleblower, a career scientist, not a political appointee, who came forward after he was suddenly reassigned after resisting orders to purchase hydroxychloroquine, the first supposed miracle cure touted by Trump. The former head of BARDA (Biomedical Advanced Research and Development Agency), the whistleblower would file a couple of weeks later, in May 2020, a formal complaint that would shine a light on the Trump administration's corruption of a public institution charged with serving public health.[7]

First, it was hydroxychloroquine; now it is chemical disinfectant, like bleach, said not only to whiten but also to brighten. Isn't it ironic? That whistleblower's name is Dr. Bright.

24
Build That Wall
The Politics of Motherhood in Portland

It is hard not to thrill at images of women saying "No" to the escalating power grabs of a president famous for saying he can "grab" women "by the pussy." In the summer of 2020, a group of women joined protests in Portland, Oregon, that had been ongoing for almost two months after the killing of a Black man, George Floyd, by police in Minnesota. Calling themselves the Wall of Moms, the women gathered in reply to a Facebook post and came out to create a barrier between vulnerable, peaceful protesters and newly arrived federal forces in their city. The forces were sent to Portland not long after Trump, who is tumbling in the polls, said that local authorities must respond to popular protests of racist police violence by "dominating the streets" and that failure to do so would mean the Feds would intervene.

One of the women in the Wall of Moms that first night was visibly pregnant. All were brave as they faced anonymized federal police forces dressed like soldiers and controlled, we found out later, by William Barr's Justice Department and Acting Secretary of Homeland Security Chad Wolfe. On their first recorded night out as a unit, July 19, 2020, the women linked arms and chanted, "Feds steer clear, Moms are here." The federal forces were ostensibly there to defend a federal courthouse that had been graffitied, but since they drove around in unmarked vans and wielded tear gas, pepper bombs, and truncheons, it seemed they were meant to serve more as accelerants than dampeners of the flames of outrage burning in Portland last summer.[1]

In the days that followed, the Moms went all in on their Mom-dom. Dressed in yellow, they sang, "Hands up, please don't shoot me," to a sing-song tune associated with lullabies or children's teasing. And they united the evenings' gathered crowds singing "One Love." They were also soon joined by the so-called Dad brigade, men wearing mostly orange t-shirts, some in hard hats, some carrying leaf-blowers, which turn out to be effective in the removal of pepper spray.

One attraction of the Portland-based Wall of Moms is that it seemed to have the requisite ironies well in hand. Calling themselves a wall, they appropriated the faux wall of the president, which promises invulnerability at the Southern border but cannot secure it. Instead of seeking that same kind of invulnerability, these women risked vulnerability alongside others and empowered each other to stand up bravely, arms linked, together and unarmed, in defiance of militarized forces in their city. Within a few days, a protest poster appeared in the crowd saying, "I'm so disappointed in you—Mom." Another addressed the federal officers: *Just wait 'til they find out your middle names. Then you will really be in for it.* It is a healing thrill for a child, even a grown child, to see the awesome power of the maternal call-out turned against an opponent. But the Mommification of the protests was also a joke about the power of the powerless: the middle name; the disappointment . . . it was all so *Mrs. America* (aka Phyllis Schlafly).

One woman came from Salem to join the Wall of Moms because she was disturbed by video she saw of a young protester hurled into a dark, unmarked van by men dressed in camo with large guns, with no pronouncement of arrest, no Miranda rights, nothing. Although there are plenty of disturbing American precedents for this type of domestic police action, including round-ups of anarchists and communists in the 1910s, '20s, '30s, and '50s, and undocumented people now, some observers of the taking of protesters by unidentified federal agents thought first of Argentina's 1970s junta and its disappearance of a generation of young, leftist protestors, thrown into cars, imprisoned, tortured, and killed. They became known as the "disappeared." It happened elsewhere, too, for example, in Chile under Pinochet.

Stuart Schrader in the *New Republic* noted the salience of the Argentine comparison: "In Argentina, death squads drove Ford Falcons, the country's most popular car, which meant that one of these sedans rolling down your street could mean you'd never see your family ever again, or it could mean nothing at all. To this day, the sight of a vintage Falcon can cause an older Argentine heart to skip a beat."[2] In Portland now, it is Dodge minivans that are repurposed for kidnappings by federal forces, and they may later suffer the same stigma as Ford in Argentina. Does Dodge know? Ford certainly did. The company provided the cars to Argentina's junta in return for union-preventing protections for their factories.

In Argentina, the disappearance of young men and women brought the Moms of that country, the Madres, into the city center, the Plaza, where they met weekly in a silent mournful protest that called for the return of the disappeared.

The Madres of the Plaza hoped to see their loved ones alive again. At the very least, they wanted to receive the bodies of their dead, if that was their fate—to bury them, to mourn them, together. That the Madres played a role in the regime's eventual downfall is undisputed. Their performance of pure maternalism forced its way into the conscience of a nation. But their activism did not subvert the traditional patriarchal politics in the name of which the junta governed. This is the irony: because the Madres exercised a specifically maternal power, they were all too easily (in the words of Diana Taylor), made "somehow marginal to the happy ending." Maternalized power is efficacious, until it isn't. After the junta was toppled, the surviving sons of the Madres took power. Were the Madres appointed to the new cabinet? No, they were sent home, because home is where moms belong.

The Wall of Moms collapsed as quickly as it ignited attention when one of its founders was found to have filed paperwork to turn the Wall of Moms into a nonprofit and another started a GoFundMe page for the group. More importantly still, the group's claims to be taking guidance from Black women leading anti-racist groups in Portland turned out to be not quite true. And the attention the mostly white women received in their brief media moment risked erasing from view the many already existing, powerful, and inspiring movements of mothers in the U.S.—for example, the Mothers of the Movement, formed after George Zimmerman was outrageously acquitted in 2013 for the murder of Trayvon Martin. In the Mothers of the Movement, Black mothers work to politicize the loss of Black life to policing. The women's maternity and their grief empower them on this issue. Over many years, they have helped energize and ground the long, slow organizing that prepared the way for the 2020 uprisings against racist police violence across the U.S. and the world. These women and the Madres of Argentina are not the same, but thinking about these two emblems of maternal politics together helps pose the question of what kinds of agency are allowed to women in politics and under what terms. The marginalization of Black women leaders in the U.S. and of the Madres in Argentina reminds us of the power and limits of maternal political agency.

A day or two before the Wall of Moms first appeared, another woman confronted the mysterious "police" forces in Portland. The *L.A. Times* referred to her as an "apparition," and there was indeed something almost supernatural in her slow, deliberate movements on the street. She had stripped naked, and, wearing only a facemask and cap, she walked, solo, from the sidewalk to the center of the street. She stood at an intersection beneath the changing red and green traffic lights and pointed her long arm to the line of unidentified men in camouflage. She did not speak. She then appeared to position herself in some yoga-like poses before sitting down on the asphalt of the street, her knees up and legs spread wide. Pussy-power, one commentator said.

When a young male protester tried to protect her with his shield, he succeeded only in drawing more fire, and she stepped away from his protection. Chivalry is dead, she seemed to say, as she killed it. She was as confident and powerful as Melisandre on *Game of Thrones*, but not evil. Faced with this one naked "No," the armed forces backed down. They got in their cars and drove away.

She was soon named Naked Athena, after the warrior virgin goddess who protected Odysseus like a son and had no children of her own. Naked Athena performed vulnerability as protest in the face of violence. She posed and sat, out in the street, with absolutely nothing on, without the cover of maternalism's performed innocence but with the protection of youthful beauty. Many initially assumed she was white and that her whiteness protected her, too, and that is likely true, though in later interviews she described herself as biracial.[3] It is fitting that she earned herself a Greek nickname, Athena, because it was she who somehow found the federal agents' Achilles' heel. All that nude pacifism was just too much for the heavily armed soldiers. The Moms, though, even before their downfall, the federal agents were willing to gas: turns out maternal authority begets not just acquiescence but also violence. Not everyone loves moms.

Incredibly, the *L.A. Times* contextualized Naked Athena's action as part of a "Portlandia" style of "quirky organic earthiness," even noting that "courts have held that appearing nude in Portland is a protected form of political expression." Having first seen an "apparition," the *L.A. Times* quickly turned it into a sitcom punchline. Why?

Because what Naked Athena did was powerful. She disturbed the registers of female agency that privilege purity and maternalize women. And so it seemed necessary to render her power scandalous, funny, or quirky: so Portland! But, rather than "Portlandia," we should contextualize her action in connection with the global feminist activism of "naked agency" in Nigeria, Ukraine, and Chile. All feature women in public, unclothed. Unlike Naked Athena, however, these women mostly appear in groups. Their power depends on their being together, they weaponize their vulnerability by appearing naked, and their determination is their focus on bringing into being a future in which women are equal and are not here to be grabbed, manipulated, or dominated.

We are also not here to be worshipped, as in some recent anti-Trump ads. In one, #NotMyChild (July 16, 2020. Don Winslow Films), a woman's relationship to her children is depicted as sacred and incomparable. "Donald Trump wants you to abandon your most primal and powerful motherly instinct to protect your child." You didn't carry them nine months to sacrifice them to the god of Covid, is more or less what a female voice-over goes on to say, as images appear of young women doting on their babies and dropping their kids at school in happier times. Keep them home, where it is safe, and vote Trump out of office for putting you in this position, the ad says. The advice seems sound. But why is it addressed to women? Men can home-school the kids, too, and watch them take their first breath, and walk their first steps. But no man appears in the ad's familial settings, as we hear the film's instruction: telling women how they feel (sacred), what to do (keep the kids home), aligning their pussy-power with the mandate of reproduction (primal, motherly). There is certainly no mention of the mommy-track effect of school closures, which have caused many women in heteronormative households to leave their jobs because with the kids home . . . well, someone has to stop working.

Such ads may be effective against Trump just as, early on, the Wall of Moms' appeals were effective in Portland. But they will have more than one kind of impact, and not all of them desirable. Anti-Trump politics can be almost as retrograde as the Trumpy men we are fighting against. The next anti-Trump ad released by Don Winslow, directly after #NotMyChild, turned from materphilia to materphobia. In #MeetMotherPence, Mike Pence's admittedly somewhat strange relationship to his wife, Karen, is the justification for representing her as ruthless in that special "mother" way we know so well from Angela Lansbury in *The Manchurian Candidate* and Hitchcock's *Psycho.* The eerily soundtracked final line of #MeetMotherPence, uttered creepily, is "A boy's best friend is his mother." In #NotMyChild that was depicted as a pure and true sentiment. In #MeetMotherPence it is a sentiment both sick and true. The lesson is not that the films are in contradiction but that maternalism is a trap, along with all its trappings (heteronormativity, the scripting of innocence as child-like, 1950s suburbanized politics).

This is why a feminism worth fighting for needs its Naked Athenas. More of them, please. I hear it takes a village. I know it takes a world, a massive cross-racial, multiethnic coalition of sexes and genders. The challenge, for the sake of that world, is to find ways to translate the vexed maternal relationships we have into progressive political power and collective action. That is the question for any "Mom"-based movements. The answer requires that we "stay together, stay tight," as the marchers in Portland say, and that "we do this every night!"

Commenting on the arrest and tear-gassing of some of the Moms in Portland, Daniel Drezner dryly noted in the *Washington Post* (July 22) that, in his experience, "radicalizing mothers is a bad political harbinger for anyone responsible. These optics are extremely unlikely to cause voters not already with Trump to shift toward him." But the question remains whether radicalizing mothers is a good political harbinger for radical mothers.

25

Impenetrable

Gaslighting the 14th Amendment

Attacking migrants as rapists and voting as theft, Trump tries to be a strongman, but the picture he paints, of a feminized America assaulted from without and within, positions him as a damsel in distress, recalling *Gaslight*'s Gregory Anton, who begins as a dominant, manipulative, controlling male but ends up feminized in the attic, nervous and nettled.[1] Tied to a chair, Gregory tries to wheedle Paula into giving him a knife that is in a drawer, just out of his reach, so that he can free himself from the ropes that bind him; so, too, Trump tries to talk Americans into freeing him, wheedling us into handing over the 14th Amendment so he can loosen the constitutional fetters that chafe and restrain him.

The 14th entrenches birthright citizenship, meaning that anyone born in the U.S. is a citizen with all the rights that go with that. This has implications, as Trump is keen to point out, for immigrants, even undocumented ones, who have children while in the U.S. Republicans call those children "anchor babies," suggesting that their parents—whether undocumented or legal immigrants—have them in order to anchor themselves in the U.S. with birthright-citizen children.

Originally, though, the 14th was intended for another class of persons: enslaved people who did not have citizenship until after the Civil War, when the 14th settled their status as free people. As Martha Jones puts it, "The Thirteenth Amendment made millions of enslaved people irretrievable and constitutionally free. But it was the Fourteenth Amendment that made them citizens."[2]

That is why Trump, and the Republican Party more generally, attack the 14th Amendment: it threatens the U.S. with what they think of as bloodmixing on two fronts, geographic and racial.[3] Trump fights back using a technique that is right out of *Gaslight*: First, hide things and then accuse others of stealing them (voting). Then, accuse others of betraying you by improperly desiring something or someone that should be out of reach (immigration, anchor babies).[4] Here is how he does it.

Trump famously called Mexicans rapists when he announced his campaign for the presidency in June 2015: "When Mexico sends its people, they're not sending their best. . . . They're bringing crime. They're rapists. And some, I assume, are good people." Again, before the 2018 midterm elections, Trump referred constantly in his rallies to the so-called caravan of migrants heading to the U.S. to escape violence and poverty at home and called them "an assault on us." Decrying rapists, Trump indicates a concern about violence against women that is surely feigned, given his own documented history.[5] As president, he defended numerous men accused of rape or assault, from Rob Porter to Brett Kavanaugh to himself, arguing they are good people, and *not* rapists. But here, he seems to say, Mexican migrants are rapists, and some of them are (also) good people? To him, migrants are rapists as such because they penetrate the U.S.

without *its* consent, and that is the one kind of rape he really does object to.[6]

In Trump's way of imagining immigration, the U.S. is the innocent victim of unwanted penetration, and all those migrants, unwanted, unwealthy, unwhite, who seek to enter the U.S. without his consent are rapists, as such. Notably, the Republican Party—the party that in the case of actual rapes is all too happy to blame the victim and ask, "What was she wearing? Didn't she ask for it?"—is not interested in looking into the role of the U.S. in creating the political and climate conditions that force people to migrate away from their homes and toward the southern border.

Since migrants sometimes have children and since those born in the U.S. are U.S. citizens, in accordance with the 14th Amendment, the crime of migration moves from rape, in Trump's imagination, to impregnation: "A woman is getting ready to have a baby, she crosses the border for one day, has the baby, all of a sudden for the next eighty years, hopefully longer, but for the next eighty years we have to take care of the people," said Trump during the 2016 campaign. "No, no, no, I don't think so." (Did he say no? Was it loud enough? Did he mean it? Okay, he said no, but maybe he meant yes? What was he wearing?) In the view promoted by Trump, the U.S.-born children of migrants are inside us *and* they have rights over us, but they shouldn't because we never consented. Shall we be forced, against our will, as a nation, to bear the children that result from this violation? Republicans think the answer is obviously "no," and they have thought so for a long time, well before Trump was numbered among their ranks. Ending birthright citizenship was much discussed at the 1996 Republican convention, and a book on the topic, *Citizenship without Consent*, widely touted.[7]

Now the very same party that opposes abortion even in cases of rape and incest is in quest of an abortifacient, willing to suspend or overrule the Constitution in order to find a way to expel the children of migrants, born here, educated here, our friends, classmates, teammates, colleagues, and neighbors.[8] (As I finalize this, Republicans are questioning the citizenship of Kamala Harris, the just-announced running mate of Joe Biden on the same grounds: her parents were immigrants. Why should their offspring count as citizens? Either she was not a citizen, it was libelously said, because it was somehow unclear whether her immigrant parents had naturalized at the time of her birth— this is not a requirement of birthright citizenship—or she was an anchor baby, a lever for securing her incredibly high-achieving parents' capacity to stay in the country.)

The 14th also says that people on the territory of the U.S., not only its citizens, have rights as well: "No state shall . . . deny to any person within its jurisdiction the equal protection of the laws." But late night round-ups and hasty deportations, not to mention forced family separations and the detainment of children, routinely violate that requirement. Worryingly, each violation is not just a violation; it is also a weakening of our norms, a wheedling that moves us one step closer to allowing the drawer to be opened and the knife taken out.

Immigrants, so often accused of taking "our jobs," are now accused of taking our suffrage (while we take their children at the border, though our taking is real and theirs a projection). But the real issue for Republicans is not foreign voting; it is domestic. The outcry about illegal voting is a way to motivate new voting restrictions aimed at minorities in the U.S. If "illegals" are voting by the thousands, as Trump said about Hillary Clinton's voters in an effort to erase his loss of the popular vote in 2016, then obviously the U.S. needs to do a better job protecting "our elections," as Trump likes to say, though what he means is *his election*.[9]

"Mr. Trump falsely claimed that millions of illegal voters cost him a popular-vote victory in 2016—but investigations, including ones by Mr. Kobach and the Justice Department under President George W. Bush, turned up scant evidence of fraud," said the *New York Times*.[10] In June 2020, more instances turned up: Trump himself may have voted illegally in Florida in 2018 and 2020 (using a non-legal residence), and several of those around him, including Kayleigh McEnany and Steve Bannon, voted illegally in Florida in the 2016 and 2018 elections. (See also Laura Ingraham, who also voted in Florida, where she was not a resident, in 2006.)

Still, in mid-May 2020, Trump went further and accused California Democrats of attempting to "steal another election. . . . It's all rigged out there. These [mail-in] votes must not count. SCAM!"[11] There is nothing furtive or forbidden about mail-in voting, which is routine in several states. These accusations further seek to establish a connection between voting and theft, now pointing not just to cagey individual fraudsters but to Democrats as Trump singles out states that currently have Democratic governors. Republican-governed states like Florida, he approvingly says, have strong absentee ballot procedures. Democratic Party–controlled states are accused of mail-in voting schemes that will defraud the system.

Notably, while we are litigating the facts, the problem has already shifted: from *illegals voting* to *illegal voting* and from the crime of rape to theft. There may be no evidence to suggest that illegal immigrants vote, but the suggestion is all that is needed to motivate new measures aimed at illegal voting, as such: like adding extra police to polling stations, creating new and often arcane rules, and prosecuting minor voting infractions.[12] All of these raise the costs of voting for citizens who have every right to vote, even making some worry it is risky, maybe too risky.

In Texas in 2016 and Georgia in 2012, two women were arrested for illegal voting. Both are Black. One, Crystal Mason, had been recently released from prison and voted while she was on probation, which she did not know is not allowed in Texas (but she consulted a poll worker and only cast a provisional ballot that was never counted). The other, Olivia Pearson, helped a first-time voter who asked for assistance figuring out how to use the machine at a polling station. Such help is assiduously monitored, when it is monitored, lest it slide into influence. The one who offers help must sign an affidavit stating the circumstances, and Pearson did this.

Crystal Mason (who, I repeat, consulted a poll worker and only cast a provisional ballot that was never counted) was found guilty and sentenced to five years in prison. Five years: just long enough to stop her voting in 2020. Olivia Pearson, who had served for eighteen years in local government, the first Black woman elected to the Douglas City Commission, was tried twice. The first trial ended with a hung jury (whose 11–1 vote suggests someone might have recently watched 12 Angry Men). The second time she was acquitted—in twenty minutes. Why did she not take a deal and instead fight so hard for so long? "Because I realize how important it is for people to vote," she said. "Because I know the history that African-Americans have had and not just African-Americans, but women, too, have had, in trying to vote."[13] Mason's lawyer had a similar take. Her client's outrageous five-year sentence was a "clarion call," she said, "to our over-policed and over-prosecuted communities of color. You are not welcome in the voting booth, and any step out of line will be punished to the fullest extent of the law."[14]

Prosecuting these individuals reinforces a structure. Make people, especially people of color, feel like voting is risky again, and they'll be more likely to stay home.[15]

Recall Paula in *Gaslight*, on the threshold of going out for a walk on a fine day, until her maid says, "Suppose the master comes back and asks where you've gone?" Is Paula *sure she* is allowed to go for a walk? Paula, already rattled, is easily made to reconsider. Trump's aim is to rattle American citizens, too, particularly people of color. In May 2020, Trump said in response to questions about his newest attacks on voting by mail that voting is an "honor."[16] It is not an honor, however, it is a right, both for those born in the U.S. and those who arrive later and are naturalized into citizenship.

But the facts may not matter. It is the affect that matters, the mood or the ambience that makes it seem, though the day is sunny, like it might rain at any moment and it might be safer to stay home. That is the aim of the rape and theft narratives directed by Republicans at the 14th Amendment. They aim to make us hesitate to cross the threshold of citizenship on Election Day. The tactics are straight out of *Gaslight*, except now the role of the housemaid who serves the master's interests is played not by Angela Lansbury, but by Fox's Laura Ingraham. In the middle of the pandemic, Ingraham urges everyone to leave their homes and risk their health in support of the president's reopening of the American economy. But come Election Day she may well sing a different tune. Don't take any chances, she may whisper: "Are you sure it's okay to go out?" We have seen the movie before, though, and so we know: if she asks, "Suppose the master comes back and asks where you've gone?," we do not need to reconsider our plans. The weather's fine, and the master will not be in charge for long.

26

"Hallelujah"

The People Want Their House Back

Using the White House to host the 2020 Republican National Convention in September, and then a rally, as well, in October, Trump took a hatchet to the Hatch Act, which forbids the use of federal government employees, properties, and resources for campaign activities. On the last night of the convention, he all but said Impeach this! as he strode down a long staircase and then strutted around a White House turned from a symbol of public government into a stage for his presidential campaign.

Trump also turned the RNC into an episode of *The Bachelor.* Casting himself in the lead role of that reality show, Trump rose above the vulnerability of electoral uncertainty. Rather than worry about whether he would be chosen (would the party choose him? Would the country?), Trump became the one who does the choosing. To whom would he give the rose, freshly plucked surely from the new made-by-Melania Rose Garden? Would the rose go to Ivanka? Or Melania? The dirty look that passed between the women after Ivanka gave her speech was straight out of one of those romance reality TV shows. So was the curved staircase on which the First Couple made their entrance, she tottering on stilettos, he—just tottering.

On the South Lawn of the White House sat 1,500 people unmasked in a pandemic defying the risks and the laws that require they sit further apart and elsewhere. Convening at the White House for a Republican Party event turned one of the seats of America's divided government into a partisan wing of a partisan party. Checks and balances are the hallmark of American government, but last night was one more peek, not our first, into what power can look like unchecked and unbalanced. With the Border Patrol Union in illegal attendance last night, in uniform, there was no one to, you know, patrol the border that is tasked with keeping governance and partisanship apart.

There were checks and balances to be had, however, albeit not from rival branches of the U.S. government. The illegal RNC speeches, music, and closing fireworks were checked and balanced by protesters who brought their own sound and light shows to the party. As RNC speaker after speaker spoke illegally at the White House, demonstrators who were gathered in Washington, D.C., edged ever closer with drums, horns, and chants to project their collective noise onto the White House lawn, protesting the taking of their public thing. Their noise—a resounding No!—rose over the only wall Trump has built during this presidency: the one that first went up during the George Floyd protests in the summer and now bunkers the White House.

The popular protest of sound was partnered with a popular protest of light. Just a few blocks away from the lawless scene at the South Lawn, the lintel of the entrance to the Trump Hotel shone with the digits "180,814," signifying the unholy number of American dead, so far, from the coronavirus pandemic. Light projection hits home without violating private property protections. This kind of graffiti does not do the kind of damage that can be prosecuted.

Trump's RNC used light, too. At the end of the evening's ceremonies, fireworks went off, and his name appeared in the sky. It was like the old Broadway producers' promise: Just imagine! Your name, up in lights! And there it was: TRUMP, all caps, lit up in the sky. But this kind of graffiti does leave a trace. The letters burned themselves out, and then tumbled in embers, to the ground below. An Icarus of writing.

Because such embers invariably fall to the ground, posing a possible risk of fire, fireworks over the Mall normally have to be approved by the government. The National Park Service approved the RNC application for fireworks a few days ago. It was one of several government enablers that supported the violation of government that night.

And that was the point, surely: the outrageous illegality of it all. The message? He is Unchained. Unbalanced. Unchecked. At one point, Trump pointed at the White House and said, "What's the name of that building?" And in case anyone missed it, he announced it: "It's not a House, it's a home," he said, meaning, it is not our House anymore, it is his home.

House, home, does it really matter? "What's in a name?," asks Juliet in Shakespeare's tragedy. "That which we call a rose, By any other name would smell as sweet." But Juliet will soon tragically learn there is no denying the power of the name. So too for us: Can it still be the White House once Trump emblazons it with his brand and makes himself at home there? Can the White House still be the building that symbolizes the revolution of a moment and the unpaid labor and the overdue justice of America's history?

More relevant still than Shakespeare, though, is Homer's *Odyssey*, in which the palace of Odysseus is taken over by would-be rivals in his absence. Odysseus is away for years, first fighting the ten-year-long Trojan War and then distracted for many years more by worldly delights and tricks as he takes the rather long way home. Summarizing Odysseus that way makes him sound a lot like a mythical version of the U.S., which has neglected its domestic obligations because too long at war and then because too long distracted from democratic work by various adventures, distractions, and delights.

The rivals who take Odysseus's place in his absence are called the suitors because they desire not only his wealth but also his wife. They are careless young men "arrogant and self-indulgent, making themselves at home" in a place that is not theirs, driven by a lust and waste so bottomless that they call to mind certain callow youths at home in the Trump Oval Office and seem to prefigure Naomi Klein's examples of neoliberal rapaciousness in *The Shock Doctrine*. But in Homer, if not in Klein, that rapaciousness extends misogynistically to wanting to take possession of Penelope, too.

Last night, Trump took the role of Homer's suitors, grabbed us all by the pussy, and announced to us, "It's my home, not your House (and, by the way, when you're president they let you do it. It's incredible)!"

So he says, but even in the old days, sometimes those who were grabbed objected. In the old days, he would quiet objectors with nondisclosure agreements, threats, denials, and payoffs. Now he sends troops into the streets to lob flash bombs, and he threatens long prison sentences that will put protestors behind Barrs, where they belong.

Earlier in the day, Joe Biden and Kamala Harris made public appearances to preview the case against Trump. Harris made note of the importance to her and to us of the sentence she would say when she used to appear in court as district attorney. "Kamala Harris, for the people." She suggested she was still "for the people" in this upcoming election. We need the representation! In court, the point of that sentence is to depersonalize the proceedings, to make it about law or justice, not vengeance. Whatever the injustices of law in the U.S., and they are many, this idea that there is a public peace that needs to be voiced, a depersonalized public thing that needs to be personated in court, is a powerful democratic idea.

Its opposite is Trump, who personalizes and privatizes everything meant to be public and shared.

Public things, like the White House, humble us as individuals with their grandeur and ennoble us as citizens. They call to us to be gathered by them into the kind of collectivities that energize democratic life. These are collectivities that go on strike in response to racial injustice, project messages on buildings to awaken people's conscience, march to protest the usurpation of a still aspirational democracy by dynasts and despots, organize free legal aid to undocumented immigrants scapegoated and rounded up, or wear masks to prevent contagion from spreading to the vulnerable.

At the end of the last evening of the RNC, they played "Hallelujah," a gorgeous song by Leonard Cohen who was certainly turning in his grave to have his work used for this purpose. The scene of the song is another palace. It belongs to another pussy-grabber with no boundaries: David, the flawed biblical king of the Israelites who slew Goliath and lusted after Bathsheba. The RNC surely hoped the song would enfold their dubious nominee in some messianic glow. But the song's glow is itself embered. "It's a cold and it's a broken Hallelujah," are its painful lyrics, since "Hallelujah" is actually a break-up song, the lament of a bereft man nothing like the television bachelor Trump wants to be.

The RNC requested permission from the Cohen estate to use his song, and they were denied. But they played it anyway, twice, performing the impunity that is their brand while calling for the law and order that was their convention theme. This is also why they used the White House for a campaign event, which is illegal, and then made a point of their illegality. Trump was reportedly delighted to have upset the libs, as they call most Americans, by using the White House as he did. It is all so sordid.

But protests, like elections, have the power to change things. Maybe the next time "Hallelujah" is played at the White House it will better suit the occasion. Marking a longed-for break-up finally secured, it could be the joyous soundtrack of the House's return to its rightful owners, we, the people, and a sad lament for all those lost on the way.

27
Loose Threads

For me literature is a way of knowing that I am not hallucinating, that whatever I feel/know is. It is an affirmation that sensuality is intelligence, that sensual language is language that makes sense.

—BARBARA CHRISTIAN

"So they urge on marriage, and I wind a skein of wiles," says Penelope to the Stranger, in Homer's *Odyssey*. She is talking partly about her nightly unraveling of the shroud she pretended to make for her father-in-law, which she told her "suitors" she must finish before considering their proposals to marry. "She set up a great loom in her palace, and set to weaving a web of threads, long and fine," says one of the suitors. "Then she said to us . . . 'now that the great Odysseus has perished, wait, though you are eager to marry me, until I finish this web.'" The shroud for Laertes was her last conjugal obligation to the household of Odysseus. For three years Penelope kept the suitors at bay by weaving all day and unraveling at night the shroud she intended never to finish.[1]

In Hannah Arendt's terms, we might say that in Penelope's hands masculinized Work—which aims to complete a discrete and lasting object—has become feminized Labor—infinite, repetitive, endless, and always to hand. Indeed, Emily Wilson says in her introduction to her new translation of the *Odyssey*, "The things Odysseus constructs (such as the Wooden Horse, his raft to get away from Calypso, and his bed) are finished, and are supposed to remain finished. Penelope's weaving is designed to be undone."[2] But perpetuity is Penelope's real product, and it works. The suitors are stalled. The great unraveling buys three years for Penelope, who will survive without compromise until Odysseus finally returns as if from the dead.[3]

It is worth risking anachronism to suggest we see Penelope as a gothic heroine. Isolated in a palace, under pressure to yield to male desire and ambition, Penelope is subjected to the shock of her home's hostile takeover by careless young men who, like Naomi Klein's neoliberal shocksters, are "so arrogant and self-indulgent, making themselves at home" in a place that is not theirs. Their lust and waste are bottomless. They want the wealth and stature of Odysseus, and they want Penelope, too.

Weaving is just one of Penelope's clever tactics, but conventional retellings of Homer's story focus more on her weaving than on her other stratagems. Perhaps this is because her weaving expresses both her cleverness and wifely fidelity to Odysseus. But, in my view, Penelope's really singular skill is not her power to weave but rather to *un*weave.[4] Every night, for three years, she finds the loose thread that will *un*ravel that day's cloth. The power to unweave is her female gothic power. Psychologically, we might say that her nightly unraveling of the cloth means that she herself will not come undone. Politically, we might say, the ability to identify the loose threads of a regime's fabric/ations is a necessary skill of citizenship. Confined to the home, Penelope offers up to politics the skill of the skein.[5]

But the skill of the skein offers more still: it is also the power to craft nonnormative kinships out of the loosened threads of patriarchal life. Penelope uses it to extend her single-woman existence for years after the end of a war in which her husband is presumed lost. When he finally returns, it is clear the war has changed him. He brings "the full force of his Iliadic fury into his own home," says Carol Dougherty, visiting a terrible violence, deserved and yet beyond measure, on the men who sought to take everything from him in his absence.[6] He will go on to slaughter almost all the suitors, but already after the first is cut down, "the bread and roasted meat were soiled with blood." We do well to consider the possibility that, after ten years at war, Odysseus suffers from PTSD. He cannot stop killing. Marriage to such a man may look less than alluring to Penelope, who nonetheless will welcome him home.

Toni Morrison says she wrote *Home* to recover Homer, and she invites us to reread the *Odyssey* alongside her novel. Like Odysseus, Homer's great hero, *Home*'s Frank Money also goes off to war and does not come straight home afterward, leaving the woman in his care, his younger sister, to the rough ways of the world, unprotected.[7] Morrison makes Frank's PTSD more explicit than Homer does Odysseus's.[8] Frank Money is described in *Home* as "discharged but still shellshocked." Morrison charts Frank's flashbacks and disorientation; his inability to resume normal life. This has the effect of highlighting the difficulty for women who must welcome home war-damaged husbands or brothers when they return from the battlefield, and this may alter our reading of Homer. Sensitized by Morrison to how women left at home have suffered their own shock and must now manage the effects of men's shell shock, too, we may now notice Homer's suggestion that Penelope is chary of Odysseus when he returns. She greets Odysseus cautiously. "You are strange," she says. Is she just not sure that he is who he says? It has been twenty years! Or might she perhaps see he is not himself? Next to *Home*'s grave depiction of Frank's postwar suffering and violence, Penelope's untold fears of Odysseus gain expression.

In *Home*, Morrison splits Homer's Penelope into two characters, both lured by the skill of the skein. The first is Lila, a woman who loves to home-make and is a master sewer. It is hard to imagine Lila unraveling anything. How could she? Her deepest desire is normative domesticity. Frank, who has fallen for her, perhaps senses he will never be part of Lila's home but only a stain upon it. He moves on. The decision to leave is precipitated by a letter calling on him to save his sister, Cee, who, as we saw in Chapter 2, suffers perilously at the hands of Dr. Beau, a white eugenicist in Georgia with a penchant for experimenting on young Black women. Cee is as homeless as Frank, having mistaken the horror-gothic suburban den of Dr. Beau for a safe refuge. Frank arrives just in time, and he takes what is left of Cee and himself back to Lotus, the tiny town where they spent their childhoods.

Cee had allowed herself, in her brother's absence, to come nearly undone. Now, secure in a real refuge, she learns her worth. A community of tough-loving women heals her, combating her shell shock with sun-smack (a kind of pussy power) and other home remedies. She regathers herself and, relatedly, she learns to quilt, gathering scraps into a thing of comfort and beauty. Later, she will proudly show Frank her first finished piece. For Cee, the skill of the skein is the capacity to sew something useful out of the tattered rags of a shell-shock experience. When the novel ends, she has made a home for herself and her brother, a nonnormative arrangement in which the brother provides and is provided for but is not a sexual or erotic partner.

In a way, Cee finishes what Penelope started. Where Penelope claims to make a shroud, but doesn't, Cee aims to sew a quilt, but it will be made into a shroud: "a shroud of lilac, crimson, yellow and dark navy blue." Later it is called "crayon-colored," as if it reaches back to her lost childhood. Cee wants to keep it or sell it, but Frank repurposes it as a gift for a father who was murdered years earlier and criminally buried in a hasty grave nearby. The violent disposal of the body was witnessed by Frank and Cee as young children, hiding frightened in the dark, and now years later, they return to the scene, unearth the man's remains, and gather them, "carefully, carefully" in Cee's first quilt, to bury him with the respect that such rituals offer, just as he deserves.[9] The Penelopean quilt is partnered with the Odyssean work of wood as Frank makes the sign to mark the grave, and it is enough. Only after that work is done can the two grown siblings finally go home.

In the AIDS era, the AIDS quilt offered a way to memorialize and humanize the dead, but, as some queer theorists noted, the quilt was also a sexually conventional, sentimental, and maternal object, more at home in heteronormative settings than in the queered spaces they had built for decades.[10] Morrison transforms the quilt's normative symbolism by affiliating Cee's quilt with chosen kinship. The buried man is no blood kin to Frank and Cee, though he is part of their history; and the siblings' life together as brother and sister, sharing a household and caring for each other as nonreproducing equals (Cee has been told she cannot bear children), is already a queer household of sorts. The quilt is very much Cee, or her childhood: scrappy, raggedy, beautiful, haphazard. It is Cee's object-self, rags once torn and discarded are regathered for a life of purpose after she nearly

died for nothing. With this happy ending, Morrison implies that conventional marriage—which both Cee and Frank have rejected—is the partner of white supremacy. Male supremacy and white supremacy are coworkers in the factory of inequality's reproduction. Find your own way. Make your own place. Practice the skill of the skein.

Dora Wheeler's *Penelope Unraveling Her Work at Night* is a needlework tapestry, silk stitched into a silk canvas whose threads are now, over a century later, frayed and stray all around. We can see the unraveling of the silk as an example of art in disrepair or as art made true to its subject. The loose threads of rationality, exceptionalism, mastery, empire, progress, masculinity, white supremacy, heteronormativity are regathered every day into sturdy fabrics that bind. They are refabricated every day. But their skeins have numerous, loose threads that escape the fabric's grasp.[11] We need to light on them and take to pulling on them to unravel these old fabrics every night. We can make of their threads something new and better. It is notable that "thread" is the term we use now on social media to indicate a longer-lasting rumination than the usual one. It is also notable that the rhapsode, one kind of ancient storyteller, is called by a Greek word that means, literally, *song-stitcher*.[12]

In a world of shock-driven flux, we long for stable things with fixity, things with the weight to counter the amorphous-ness and the detail to cut through the daily deluge. It was such a longing that led me to offer toward the beginning of this volume not a rumination on gaslighting the phenome-non (that came later) but first, and foremost, a reading of the film *Gaslight*.[13] Where gaslighting has become for us the name for a host of behaviors like those of the evil husband, Gregory Anton, the gaslight was also Paula's tether to reality, and she clung to it. As it inexplicably waxed and waned, it was a source of both torment and hope. Embedded in the film, then, was the kind of detail to which feminist criticism itself clings. That this particular detail is also a device of illumination is fitting.

Indeed, it seems important that the film opens with a lamplighter, presumably working for the city, who lights the gaslights in the streets as darkness falls. He too is a gaslighter, but this gaslighter is the opposite of the evil one. Rather than deprive us of the knowledge of our senses, he provides the conditions needed for us to rely on them more fully. Those streetlights, and the man who lights them, are public things. They are what the shock politics of neoliberalization and misogyny try to wipe out. The work of the good gaslighter reasserts, it does not undo, the power of public things to provide the worldly orientation that citizenship requires. With him on the job, the streets are safe: it is only the domain of the household that threatens to go noir.[14] We know better, however. A whole country can go noir, espe-cially if the public and its servants have been shrunk in recent decades and if, increasingly, those that remain are, like Anton's two compromised housemaids, protected by feudal-like loyalties. When a democracy is deprived of the key points of orientation that proper public things, formal offices, and distinguished public service can provide, we are thrust into the shock politics two-step. Too often, the racism and misogyny we live with every day thrive there.

When Hannah Arendt says (as we saw in Chapter 2) that Locke's empiricism is not enough, that our senses must be underwritten by a sixth sense, the common sense, she means to certify sensorial experience as a worldly experience, not to conjure the sixth sense of extrasensory perception, or E.S.P. But in a world of privatization, it may take a turn to the extrasensory, surely at least to the imagination, to conjure the common that Arendt, a Jewish refugee from Nazi Germany, knew we could not take for granted. Hence Arendt's own turn to literature, and hence feminist criticism's turn to literature, TV, and film. But we can follow the loose thread of the sixth sense even further. In the film *The Sixth Sense*, a child with special powers says, "I see dead people."[15] (Like Morrison's Cee, his name too puns on sight: Cole Sear.) The dead people, Sear comes to learn, are ghosts who have "unfinished business" with the world, and he overcomes his fears to respond to their calls for justice. It turns out his extrasensorial sixth sense is both the common sense to which Arendt resorted—justice should be done— and an extrasensory sensitivity to what the common sense has all too often denied: its historical implication in injustice, both blind and willful.

The hope of feminist criticism is that the grounding practice of close reading can help counter the shock politics two-step, that wild connections can resensitize the senses, and that the orienting power of public things can center our efforts to take care of American democracy's unfinished business. It is a plank of American white supremacy to deny the evidence of our senses and to barrage us with platitudes about how we are all equal under the law, while Black Americans are disproportionately policed, criminalized, injured, imprisoned, and killed by law enforcement and while women are disbelieved when they've been assaulted or harassed. When such violations are attributed to so-called "bad apples," the sensory feeling that something larger is going on is dismissed as paranoid. Paula, you're imagining things, says Gregory Anton pityingly to his shell-shocked wife. These are the words of whiteness to its others: "Why do you keep making everything about race?"[16] Patriarchy chimes in: "But are you sure he meant it that way? Aren't you exaggerating? Or imagining?" It is all so like that children's "game" in which someone grabs holds of your wrists and moves them so you are made to slap your own face with your own hands as you are taunted: why do you keep hitting yourself?

Why, indeed.

The unraveling and regathering prized by feminist criticism are enabled by the detective skills, moral determination, powers of repair, and a sixth sense–style sensitivity to those who haunt our present with their "unfinished business." Such loose threads are well met with the skill of the skein, whose virtues are demonstrated by Penelope in Homer, Cee in *Home*, Paula in *Gaslight*, the mother Joyce Byers in *Stranger Things*, the two women detectives in *Unbelievable*, and, in the real world of contemporary American politics, Frederica Wilson, Maxine Waters, Fiona Hill, Christine Blasey Ford, Ana Maria Archila, Maria Gallagher, Pamela Karlan, Elin Ersson, Stephanie Wilkinson, Crystal Mason, Olivia Pearson, Yamiche Alcindor, Naked Athena, and the national Mothers of the Movement. Their stories can light the streets of a more just future.

For some, it takes courage, above all, to envision what else might be; for others desperation is the driver. Either way, speaking out and acting up light up this possibility. We respond to the shock two-step of sensorial deprivation and saturation with close reading and our own two-step: the unraveling and regathering of political action plus joy. This is an Arendtian idea: when we join with others in care for the world, our action in concert with diverse others generates collective power and brings with it the pleasure of appearing in the world with others in common cause.

I have suggested we call it a Politics That Sustains Democracy, proposing a new PTSD take the place of the shock politics version. The counter to the shock two-step detailed by Naomi Klein is a different two-step: exposé (which draws on the forensic powers of the gaslit and shell shocked) and joy (drawing on Hannah Arendt's account of the experience of acting in concert). A Politics That Sustains Democracy demands infrastructures of collective sustenance and shared sensation. Public things are part of that infrastructure, and so are stories. Stories store the energies of past events for future expenditure; and feminist criticism revels in them, rubbing their fabric, testing their weight, pulling on their loose threads. The hope is to regenerate neural networks severed by shock and offer the comfort or compass of details and objects we can cling to in the disarray, like Odysseus to what is left of his raft, lest we despair. Feminist critics tell the stories we might otherwise have missed or retell those whose precious details we missed, shedding new light, showing new possibilities, cracking a surface so the light gets in, and the dark, too. Listening daily and in detail to the pain and pleasure in each other's voices, gathered around, our senses are honed for the nightly unraveling, our empathy becomes practiced, our vision is sharpened, our spirits are uplifted, and we are regathered for the long days ahead.

Acknowledgments

I am grateful to Lori Marso, Jill Frank, Corey Robin, Bruce Robbins, Jeff Tulis, George Shulman, Libby Anker, Robert Corber, Jeff Masten, Joe Litvak, Lawrence Glickman, Tricia Rose, Andre Willis, Richard Locke, Nancy L. Buc, Wendy Ferenc, Melanie Simon, Davide Panagia, Stephen Merkel, Michael Whinston, Naomi Honig, and Noah Whinston, who encouraged me to go public and/or commented on or inspired some of the pieces here. The virtual communities of Facebook friends and then MeWe did, too. One of the chapters included here is coauthored with Sara Rushing, a Facebook friend at the time and political theorist whom I do not know in real life. Through social media, we ventured into an accidental coauthorship that made us (and, I hope, others) laugh, while learning something from the uncanny coincidence of the names of Jeffrey Epstein and William Barr with the Epstein-Barr virus. That virus cannot be cured, only managed. The same may be true for some of the ills that have long afflicted American democratic institutions.

Thank you to Amanda Anderson, who read the whole thing at the last minute and responded with characteristic insight and encouragement.

Marc Stears asked me to share an early version of the "Gaslight" chapter (which turned into two chapters, the second and the last, on *Gaslight* and on Homer's Penelope) in the winter/summer of 2020 with his great team at the University of Sydney Policy Lab and at a wonderful event for community activists and local organizers. Thank you to all involved. Just as I thought I was done, Jonathon Catlin invited me to present work from this project at Princeton's Interdisciplinary Doctoral Program in the Humanities (IHUM) Humanities Center, which led me to develop in more detail parts of the argument in those same two chapters.

And thanks to Deirdre Foley for help acquiring and preparing the images for publication and to Ferris Lupino and Claire Grandy for help preparing the manuscript for publication.

This volume features several brand-new pieces written for this collection. All the rest are revised versions—most almost entirely rewritten and updated—of work that appeared first in the *Boston Review,* the *Los Angeles Review of Books, Politicsslashletters,* Australia's *ABC Religion and Ethics* website, and the *Contemporary Condition* blog. I want to thank Joshua Cohen and Deb Chasman for the good work of the *Boston Review,* Katie Fitzpatrick and Ellie Duke, who worked with me at LARB, Bruce Robbins at *Politicsslashletters,* and Jairus Grove at the *Contemporary Condition* for their incredible and quick turnarounds. Bruce—to whom I dedicate this book—is an especially keen-eyed editor, generous interlocutor, and empathic soul. Jairus is magic at finding the right images. The *Contemporary Condition* exists because Bill Connolly and others wisely saw early on how important it was to provide critical political theory with a room of its own on the web. Bill was also the very first to urge me to turn a brief FB comment into a more considered blog post.

Finally, a few people, early on, encouraged me to pursue this project: Davide Panagia, Lori Marso, Bruce Robbins, Angela Chnapko, and Libby Anker. Bill McNeil's support bought me the time I needed to get it done. At Fordham, Thomas Lay embraced the book and provided the kind of editorial guidance I had thought was a thing of the past. For that, especially, I am very grateful.

Notes

1. Trump's Family Romance and the Magic of Television

1. Donald J. Trump and Tony Schwartz, *Trump: The Art of the Deal* (New York: Random House, 1987), 79–80. To this day, Trump does not look up during his executive time, watching TV. And his constant tweeting and floating of teasers to the public about what may happen next is him refusing to "turn it off."

2. The Mueller Report was on Russian interference in the 2016 presidential election and the Trump campaign's involvement in that. On Schwarzenegger, see Jude Dry, "Arnold Schwarzenegger Says Donald Trump Is 'In Love with' Him, 'Wants to Be' Him," *IndieWire*, September 10, 2019, https://www.indiewire.com/2019/09/schwarzenegger-trump-in-love-apprentice-1202172399/. Trump judges everyone by TV standards—on Twitter he is a TV critic—and he invites everyone else to do the same. About Mueller he said, "The performance was obviously not very good. He had a lot of problems. But what he showed more than anything else is that this whole thing has been three years of embarrassment and waste of time for our country." He was reported to have taken particular "note of Mr. Mueller's physical appearance and halting response to some questions," and he also said, "I think Robert Mueller did a

horrible job, both today and with respect to the investigation," and "Obviously he did very poorly today. I don't think there's anybody—even among the fakers—I don't think there's anybody that would say he did well"; Michael D. Shear and Lola Fadulu, "Trump Says Mueller Was 'Horrible' and Republicans 'Had a Good Day,'" *New York Times*, June 24, 2019, https://www.nytimes.com/2019/07/24/us/politics/trump-mueller.html. This dismissal of Mueller on the basis of telegenics stands in counterpoint to the claim by Harry Sandick, a former assistant U.S. attorney in the Southern District of New York, quoted in the *Guardian*: "Prosecutors aren't television hosts. They're not entertainers, and they should do their talking in the courtroom and in their court filings. It's not their job to wage the battle of public opinion. It's their job to investigate and prosecute crimes"; Tom McCarthy, "Trump v Mueller: How the President won the Messaging Wars," *Guardian*, June 11, 2019, https://www.theguardian.com/us-news/2019/jun/11/robert-mueller-trump-russia-investigation. Calling Trump a "televisual thinker," James Poniewozik notes the significance of Trump's expressed appreciation, in Tulsa, in June 2020, for the many televisions on Air Force One ("Onscreen the Trump Campaign Ramps Up, and Down," *New York Times*, June 22, 2020).

3. TV is an assemblage. If Trump's mother was empowered that day, it was as a member of an empire-wide community into which she was interpellated by the broadcast as she watched it along with millions of others worldwide.

4. For Freud's views on family romance, see Sigmund Freud, "Family Romances," *Ricorso*, 1909, http://www.ricorso.net/rx/library/criticism/guest/Freud_S/Freud_S3.htm. The family romance is a stage, a trait suited to a certain age. If it becomes a lifelong state, it is a delusion of grandeur. This may offer some perspective on the grandiose decorations and modes of familial photography used by Trump in his tower.

5. That is, by way of a kind of contiguity and psychic transfer that may be all that is meant by the "magic of TV." In the watching of the watching, we may hear resonances of *Rear Window*, in production that very year and released in 1954.

6. Pamela S. Karlan, "House Impeachment Inquiry—Feldman, Karlan, Gerhardt & Turley Testimony," C-SPAN, December 4, 2019, YouTube video, 9:03:28, https://youtu.be/MUSQaYHJAiI.

7. Callum Borchers, "The Amazing Story of Donald Trump's Old Spokesman, John Barron—Who Was Actually Donald Trump Himself," *Washington Post*, May 13, 2016, https://www.washingtonpost.com/news/the-fix/wp/2016/03/21/the-amazing-story-of-donald-trumps-old-spokesman-john-barron-who-was-actually-donald-trump-himself/.

8. Emily Stewart, "The Manufactured Outrage over Barron Trump, Explained," *Vox*, December 5, 2019, https://www.vox.com/policy-and-politics/2019/12/5/20996885/barron-trump-pamela-karlan-impeachment-hearing-baron-joke.

9. "Southerners at the convention insisted that their slaves be counted when allocating representation in Congress, even though everyone understood that slaves were considered property and had no political rights." The irony is bitter: representation for enslaved people added to the power of slaveowners to keep them enslaved. The moral offense was well observed by Gouverneur Morris (from New York, and representing Pennsylvania at the Constitutional Convention), who said, "The inhabitant of Georgia and South Carolina who goes to the Coast of Africa, and in defiance of the most sacred laws of humanity tears away his fellow creatures from their dearest connections and damns them to the most cruel bondages, shall have more votes in a Government instituted for protection of the rights of mankind, than the Citizen of Pennsylvania or New Jersey who views with a laudable horror, so nefarious a practice"; Paul Finkelman, "Three-Fifths Clause: Why Its Taint Persists," *Root*, February 26, 2013, https://www.theroot.com/three-fifths-clause-why-its-taint-persists-1790895387.

10. Saikrishna Bangalore Prakash, "Stop Fighting It. America Is a Monarchy, and That's Probably for the Best," *Washington Post*, June 23, 2015, https://www.washingtonpost.com/posteverything/wp/2015/06/23/stop-fighting-it-america-is-a-monarchy-and-thats-probably-for-the-best/.

11. Emily Bazelon, "What Happens When a President and Congress Go to War?," *New York Times Magazine*, November 5, 2019, https://www.nytimes.com/2019/11/05/magazine/congress-president-impeachment.html. It is worth noting the willingness with which the legislative branch has given up power, especially since 9/11, for political reasons.

12. The idea of distinguishing theory and criticism in such a way was first suggested to me by Amanda Anderson's great "Criticism and Theory: 22 Theses," *Politicsslashletters*, January 8, 2019, http://politicsslashletters.org/commentary/criticism-and-theory-22-theses/. Then, among other things on the topic, I read Barbara Christian's inspiring and illuminating essay, "The Race for Theory."

13. Naomi Klein, *The Shock Doctrine: The Rise of Disaster Capitalism* (Toronto: Alfred A. Knopf Canada, 2007).

14. Bethania Palma, "Did Trump Say Crashing the Economy Would Get People Back to Work?," *Snopes*, January 6, 2017, https://www.snopes.com/fact-check/trump-economy-crashing-quote/.

15. "Over fourteen seasons, the television producer Mark Burnett helped turn the Donald Trump of the late nineties—the disgraced huckster who had trashed Atlantic City; a tabloid pariah to whom no bank would lend—into a titan of industry, nationally admired for being, in his own words, the highest-quality brand"; Emily Nussbaum, "The TV That Created Donald Trump," *New Yorker*, July 24, 2017, https://www.newyorker.com/magazine/2017/07/31/the-tv-that-created-donald-trump.

16. Walter Benjamin, "The Author as Producer," in *The Work of Art in the Age of Its Technological Reproducibility and Other Writings on Media*, ed. Michael W. Jennings, Brigid Doherty, and Thomas Y. Levin, trans. Edmund Jephcott et al. (Cambridge, Mass.: Belknap, 2008), 79–95.

17. Karlan, "House Impeachment Inquiry—Feldman, Karlan, Gerhardt & Turley Testimony."

18. Michelle Goldberg, "Trump to Governors: I'd Like You to Do Us a Favor, Though," *New York Times*, March 30, 2020, https://www.nytimes.com/2020/03/30/opinion/trump-federal-aid-coronavirus.html.

19. Later, with over 90,000 Americans dead of Covid-19, Trump again erased a woman's name when he charged that states providing their citizens with the opportunity to vote by mail were cheating somehow: "Breaking: Michigan sends absentee ballots to 7.7 million people ahead of Primaries and the General Election. This was done illegally and without authorization by a rogue Secretary of State. I will ask to hold up funding to Michigan if they want to go down this Voter Fraud path!," he said, reprising the quid pro quo he was accused of with Ukraine. In fact, the secretary of state had sent out not ballots but *applications to vote by mail*, as she herself said in a reply on Twitter: "Hi! I also have a name, it's Jocelyn Benson. And we sent applications, not ballots. Just like my GOP colleagues in Iowa, Georgia, Nebraska and West Virginia." Trump deleted his first tweet mentioning ballots and posted another tweet, otherwise the same as the first. Benson responded again: "Every Michigan registered voter has a right to vote by mail. I have the authority & responsibility to make sure that they know how to exercise this right—just like my GOP colleagues are doing in GA, IA, NE, and WV. Also, again, my name is Jocelyn Benson." Jocelyn Benson understands the name game, the dynamic in which the man who puts his own name on everything will not use the names of those he combats in public. Some get nicknames (Nervous Nancy, Shifty Schiff) and others lose their names entirely: "the woman from Michigan," the "rogue Secretary of State," and so on. https://www.factcheck.org/2020/05/ trumps-false-tweet-about-michigan-absentee-ballot-applications/.

20. This extends Republican ballot harvesting to word harvesting; Robert Mackey, "In Exchange for Aid, Trump Wants Praise from Governors He Can Use in Campaign Ads," *Intercept*, March 28, 2020, https://theintercept.com/2020/03/28/exchange -aid-trump-wants-praise-governors-can-use-campaign-ads/.

2. *Gaslight* and the Shock Politics Two-Step

1. Naomi Klein, "How Big Tech Plans to Profit from the Pandemic," *Guardian*, May 13, 2020, https://www.theguardian .com/news/2020/may/13/naomi-klein-how-big-tech-plans-to-profit -from-coronavirus-pandemic.

2. Klein, "Resources: Part 7, Chapter 19: Blanking the Beach," accessed June 20, 2020, http://tsd.naomiklein.org/shock-doctrine/resources/part7/chapter19.

3. Klein could have gone back earlier, to the use, in London during WWI, of similar techniques to heal/torture soldiers suffering from shell shock and return them to the front. The historically based novel *Regeneration* reports on the use of shock by Dr. Lewis Yealland, who used "frequent and agonising electrical shocks to a patient who has been made mute by his experiences at the front. The terrified soldier must utter words to get the torture to stop" (John Mullan, "Regeneration *by Pat Barker*," *The Guardian*, Aug. 24, 2012. https://www.theguardian.com/books/2012/aug/24/book-club-pat-barker-regeneration). In Montreal, Cameron later tried depatterning to cure schizophrenia. In a coauthored paper in *Comprehensive Psychiatry* (1962), he favored using "a combination of electroshock, barbiturates and sensory deprivation to disrupt patients' sense of time and space" (see Naomi Klein, Disaster Capitalism in Action Archive, Part 1, Chapter 1: The Torture Lab at http://tsd.naomiklein.org/files/resources/pdfs/depatterning.pdf).

4. In a review of Klein's book, Joe Stiglitz calls her comparison of economic and neurological shock therapies "overdramatic and unconvincing," a phrasing that could itself be subjected to a gendered analysis. Stiglitz seems to think Klein claims a causal connection between neurological and economic shock, or that she conflates them, but I see her as offering an instructive juxtaposition for our moment of shock politics, which has its own unique markers in the context of neoliberalism and patriarchy, respectively; Joseph E. Stiglitz, "Bleakonomics," *New York Times*, September 30, 2007, https://www.nytimes.com/2007/09/30/books/review/Stiglitz-t.html.

5. Klein notes how the deprivation of normal sensory stimulation makes people long for, even crave, stimulation; so too the civic body deprived of the stimulations of public things and public life seems to long for its lost stimulations and, in quest of replacements, will embrace what is on offer.

6. On flooding the zone, see Sean Illing, "'Flood the Zone with Shit': How Misinformation Overwhelmed Our Democracy," *Vox*, February 6, 2020, https://www.vox.com/platform/amp/policy-and-politics/2020/1/16/20991816/impeachment-trial-trump-bannon-misinformation. The 2003 invasion of Iraq by the U.S. featured the same two-step: first, the destruction by the U.S. of Iraqi telephone communications and, then, the use of sonic bombs in Iraq, respectively, with the effect, first, of depriving and then, second, overwhelming the audial sense.

7. In *The Shock Doctrine*, Naomi Klein identifies three moments in the practice of shock: First, the crisis, which may be a political event (a coup) or a natural one (earthquake), followed by the use of that event to introduce in an overwhelming way novelty, not recovery (clean slates are opportunities!), and then the use of torture, including electric shocks, practiced on the bodies of those who resist. I refer here to the shock two-step, not three, because torture can be seen not as a third distinct step but as an intensification of the first two. Elaine Scarry's *The Body in Pain* highlights the deliberate desensitizing aims of torture and the resulting loss of language as loss of world; Scarry, *The Body in Pain* (New York: Oxford University Press, 1985).

8. Carol D. Leonnig and Philip Rucker, "'You're a Bunch of Dopes and Babies': Inside Trump's Stunning Tirade against Generals," *Washington Post*, January 17, 2020, https://www.washingtonpost.com/politics/youre-a-bunch-of-dopes-and-babies-inside-trumps-stunning-tirade-against-generals/2020/01/16/d6dbb8a6-387e-11ea-bb7b-265f4554af6d_story.html.

9. *Gaslight*, directed by George Cukor (MGM, 1944), DVD.

10. For Paula, that is, by contrast with Jane, there is every possibility of going for a walk that day, but Paula starts and then returns: "It looks as if it might rain . . . so I thought I should have my umbrella." Something brings back her own uncertainty, and it is not just about the weather. "Of course, ma'am. Suppose the master comes back and asks where you've gone?" "Tell him I just went for a walk." "By yourself, ma'am?" "Of course. Why not?" "Suppose the master asks where?" "Tell him I just . . ."; *Gaslight*.

11. Such details are the loose threads to which feminist criticism returns. But clinging to such details can be "tedious," as Michelle Goldberg points out in her March 19, 2020, *New York Times* op ed: "It can become tedious to dwell on the fact that the president is a dangerous and ignorant narcissist who has utterly failed as an executive, leaving state governments on their own to confront a generational cataclysm. But no one should ever forget it"; Goldberg, "Of Course Trump Deserves Blame for the Coronavirus Crisis," *New York Times*, March 19, 2020, https://www.nytimes.com/2020/03/19/opinion/trump-coronavirus-us.html.

12. Locke's *Essay* (3.3.7). Insisting that we rely only on our own senses, he sets aside perspectivism and (classed) plurality, the ethical and political conditions of seeing a shared world from another's perspective; John Locke, "Book III," in *An Essay Concerning Human Understanding, Early Modern Texts*, http://earlymoderntexts.com/assets/pdfs/locke1690book3.pdf.

13. Focused on feminization, this collection tacks between race, class, and gender, but on race and gaslighting, in particular, see "Racial Gaslighting," the 2019 essay by Angelique M. Davis and Rose Ernst: "We define racial gaslighting as the political, social, economic and cultural process that perpetuates and normalizes a white supremacist reality through pathologizing those who resist"; Davis and Ernst, *Politics, Groups, and Identities* 7, no. 4 (2019): 761–74.

14. Hannah Arendt, *The Human Condition*, 2nd ed. (Chicago: University of Chicago Press, 1998), 208–9.

15. For discussion of Arendt's relevance to media studies today, see *World Records* special issue on Hannah Arendt and documentary media: "'In the Presence of Others': Hannah Arendt and Documentary," *World Records*, accessed June 18, 2020, https://worldrecordsjournal.org/volume-four/.

16. The enlistment of the female household staff in *Gaslight* resonates with the story of Penelope, to which I turn later. Penelope tries to stall would-be suitors from forcing her into marriage, but she is betrayed "verily by the help of my maidens, disrespectful bitches. . . . And now I can neither escape the marriage nor devise any counsel more"; Homer, *The Odyssey*,

trans. A. T. Murray (Cambridge, Mass.: Harvard University Press, 1919), Perseus Digital Library, http://www.perseus.tufts.edu/hopper/text?doc=urn:cts:greekLit:tlg0012.tlg002.perseus-eng1. And, of course, in *Bombshell*'s true story, also discussed later in this volume, Roger Ailes's secretary is the older woman who is part of the "honeypot" named as such in the case of Harvey Weinstein. Her presence reassures the unsuspecting and helps lure them into the lair.

17. The *pretense of a social egalitarianism* that interests a man not at all is a good description of Trump and his much-proclaimed commitment to the "forgotten man," whom he is first to forget and whose celebration is really an occasion for the degradation of nearly everyone else. Thanks to Libby Anker on this point.

18. The house that was Paula's and is now Anton's becomes in the film *Get Out* (a racial gothic) the body that once belonged to a kidnapped Black person and is now taken for their own personal use by whites. The crime of taking Black bodies for white use is the central motif of gothic capture in Morrison's *Home* (New York: Vintage International, 2013) as well, as we shall see.

19. Oddly, though he works for Scotland Yard, Cotten's Cameron makes no effort to disguise his American accent, which contrasts sharply with the European accents of Anton and Paula, played by Charles Boyer and Ingrid Bergman, and the various English accents of almost everyone else in the film. Perhaps the choice is deliberate, a way to subtly position American innocence as a counter to the guilt of a then war-torn Europe. Anton is said to be from Prague, and the film is set in London. (In the earlier British version of the film, Anton's character's real name is Louis Bauer. In the American version, he becomes Sergis Bauer, more central European.) Certainly, Cameron's plainspoken pragmatism and proper legalism code "American" by contrast with what we might take to be the mystifications of Anton's Europeanism.

20. On how to make sense of the seeming vicious circularity of truths holding us and we holding them in the Declaration of Independence, see Bonnie Honig, "Declarations of Independence: Arendt and Derrida on the Problem of Founding a Republic" in *American Political Science Review*, March 1991.

21. We return to this point later, in my reading of the film 12 *Angry Men*, where we see how care for public things and the racial politics thereof are part of the story we see here.

22. The domineering man is also always quick to claim he is victimized: See, for example, Amanda Marcotte on the Senate impeachment trial: "White House lawyers . . . simply used their time to declare that Trump is a victim and, by the transitive property of right-wing aggrievement, that the entire Trump base is a great mass of victims. 'They're not here to steal one election, they're here to steal two elections,' Cipollone declared, claiming that Democrats were trying to 'deny the American people the right to vote.' (If you're keeping score, that would literally be the opposite of the truth.) Cipollone is simply imitating his client, a relentless practitioner of the psychological concept known as 'projection,' sometimes known as 'DARVO,' short for 'Deny, Attack, and Reverse Victim and Offender.' In interpersonal relationships, this is what abusers do to squash their victims' attempts to resist, by flinging accusations that the victim is the real victimizer"; Amanda Marcotte, "Trump's Lawyers Make Their Case: White-Dude Whining and Persecution Fantasies," *Salon*, January 22, 2020, https://www.salon.com/2020/01/22/trumps -lawyers-make-their-case-white-dude-whining-and-persecution -fantasies/.

23. Viewers of Netflix's *Stranger Things*, Season 1, will recognize the shock two-step. Eleven, the young girl held captive by government agents who want to exploit her extrasensory powers, is put into an "isolation tank" in which you "lose any sense of sense and feel nothing and see nothing." This sensory deprivation is followed by sensory saturation when Eleven, still in the tank, confronts the monster from which she has been ordered not to look away and is overwhelmed; *Stranger Things*, created by Matt Duffer and Ross Duffer (21 Laps Entertainment, 2016), Netflix.

24. On her supposed madness in the context of Jamaican and English plantation slavery, see Sue Thomas, "The Tropical Extravagance of Bertha Mason," *Victorian Literature and Culture* 27, no. 1 (1999): 1–17, https://www.jstor.org/stable/pdf/25058436

.pdf. The key text for a worldly reading of *Jane Eyre* is Gayatri
Chakravorty Spivak, "Three Women's Texts and a Critique of
Imperialism," *Critical Inquiry* 12, no. 1 (Autumn 1985): 243–61.
Spivak argues powerfully that Jane is moved from "counter-
family" to "family-in-law" by the "unquestioned ideology of
imperialist axiomatics." Race, class, and empire all play a role. I
cannot detail it here, but the same is true in *Home*, where Frank
Money's time as a U.S. soldier in Korea is interlaced with his
experiences of racism at home.

   25. Uncannily, since she arrives to the Rivers family in a state
of shock and recovers in their care, the name "Rivers" belongs
also to the real, not fictional, W. H. R. Rivers, who famously
treated sufferers of WWI shell shock, with a focus on the
sensorial damage of war and pursuing humanistic recovery like
talk therapy, time in natural surroundings, art, and poetry.
W. H. R. Rivers is not mentioned in Klein's book, but he is the
hero of *Regeneration*, Pat Barker's fictionalized version of the
story. Regeneration refers also to an experiment in nerve damage
conducted by Rivers well before WWI, in 1903. Charting the two
stages of nerve regeneration, he and his colleague, Henry Head
(on whom the experiment was performed) called this first stage
of the recovery process *protopathic*, noting "either an inordinate
response to sensation when compared with normal reaction or
no reaction whatever." The next stage of healing, called "epicritic,"
from the Greek *epikritikos*, meaning "determinative," involved
further resensitization and connection: "Precision improves in
localizing a stimulus which is now felt as sharp but not painful
and pointed rather than diffuse." Pain is now felt in the same
spot as where the needle pricks the skin and not, as in stage 1, in
some other dislocated place. Thus, in stage 2 the reality of the
pain is shared with and guaranteed by others. This is where the
two researchers see that "sense of position in space [or] spacial
[*sic*] discrimination depends on the activity of the epicritic
system only"; Alastair Compston, "A Human Experiment in
Nerve Division by W. H. R. Rivers MD FRS, Fellow of St
John's College Cambridge and Henry Head MD FRS, Physician
to the London Hospital, *Brain* 31 (1908): 323–450," *Brain* 132,

no. 11 (November 2009): 2903–5. The epicritic is the stage at which, I want to say, Arendtian common sense takes hold again as the experiences of pain from inside and outside line up together. Thus, we may think of feminist criticism as a kind of epi*criticism*.

26. Spivak, "Three Women's Texts and a Critique of Imperialism," 243–61.

27. Morrison, *Home*, 60.

28. Ibid., 112.

29. Ibid., 65.

30. Ibid., 128.

31. Ibid., 119.

32. Ibid., 121, 126, and 129.

33. Ibid., 131. For one piece of the relevant history of eviction and racial terror in the context of which the women of *Home* know the truth and keep on gardening, see Mark Ellis, "Racial Unrest and White Liberalism in Rural Georgia: Barrow and Oconee Counties in the Early 1920s," *Georgia Historical Quarterly* 97, no. 1 (Spring 2013): 45.

34. Daphne du Maurier, *Rebecca* (New York: Doubleday, 1953), 375.

35. Ibid., quoted in Honig, *Democracy and the Foreigner*, 113. For more on maternalization as a patriarchal tactic, see Honig, *A Feminist Theory of Refusal* (Cambridge, Mass.: Harvard University Press, 2021).

36. The fabric of the in-between is a figure for the object permanence provided by the domain of life that Hannah Arendt calls Work. From carpentry to art and poetry, Work's fabrications punctuate and stabilize a world that is either too fast-moving (action) or endlessly repeating (labor).

3. The President's House Is Empty: Inauguration Day

1. The costs were huge, and the benefits incalculable. The *Washington Post* reported in June 2020 that when "Melania Trump stayed behind in New York after her husband's presidential inauguration, she said it was because she didn't want to interrupt their then-10-year-old son Barron's school year. News stories at

the time concentrated on an apparent frostiness between the first couple and on the exorbitant taxpayer costs to protect Melania and Barron away from Washington." It is more recently suggested that "the first lady was also using her delayed arrival to the White House as leverage for renegotiating her prenuptial agreement with President Trump." In the end, the more conventional arrangement of the First Family living in the White House was adopted. By mid-2018, "Melania had finally renegotiated the prenup to her liking. She had already been looking out for Barron's future by making sure he had dual citizenship in Slovenia, which will position him to work in Europe for the Trump Organization when he comes of age"; Jada Yuan, "Melania Trump Was in No Rush to Move into the White House. That's When She Renegotiated Her Prenup, a New Book says"; *Washington Post*, June 12, 2020, https://www .washingtonpost.com/lifestyle/melania-book-art-of-her-deal -prenup-white-house/2020/06/11/ce63ec02-abec-11ea-94d2-d7bc 43b26bf9_story.html.

2. David A. Fahrenthold and Joshua Partlow, "Trump's Company Has Received at Least $970,000 from U.S. Taxpayers for Room Rentals," *Washington Post*, May 14, 2020, https://www .washingtonpost.com/politics/trumps-company-has-received-at -least-970000-from-us-taxpayers-for-room-rentals/2020/05/14/26 d27862-916d-11ea-9e23-6914ee41oa5f_story.html.

3. Julia Marsh, "Trump Tower Security May Take Over 2 Floors—and Cost Millions," *New York Post*, November 2016, https://nypost.com/2016/11/24/trump-tower-security-may-take -over-2-floors-and-cost-millions/.

4. However, three years after this essay was first drafted, we now see battles over public statuary commemorating heroes of the so-called Lost Cause, which reveal an ongoing investment in public things.

4. He Said, He Said: The Feminization of James Comey

1. Bobby Lewis, "Conservative Media Deflect from James Comey's Testimony by Attacking His Sexuality and Gender," *Media Matters*, June 8, 2017, https://www.mediamatters.org/laura

-ingraham/conservative-media-deflect-james-comeys-testimony
-attacking-his-sexuality-and-gender.

2. Nicole Serratore, "James Comey and the Predator in Chief,"
New York Times, June 8, 2017, https://www.nytimes.com/2017/06/
08/opinion/james-comey-and-the-predator-in-chief.html.

3. Eliza Relman, "Comey Said He Wishes He Had Kept a
Date with His Wife Instead of Having Dinner with Trump,"
Business Insider, June 8, 2017, https://www.businessinsider.com/
comey-wife-date-trump-white-house-dinner.

4. In 2020, Tom Nichols would call Trump "The Most
Unmanly President" and wonder how and why real men would
support someone whose masculinity is so faux and wanting.
"Whenever he is in the company of Russian President Vladimir
Putin, to take the most cringe-inducing example, he visibly
cowers. His attempts to ingratiate himself with Putin are
embarrassing, especially given how effortlessly Putin can bend
Trump to his will. When the Russian leader got Trump alone at
a summit in Helsinki, he scared him so badly that at the
subsequent joint press conference, Putin smiled pleasantly while
the president of the United States publicly took the word of a
former KGB officer over his own intelligence agencies"; Nichols,
"Donald Trump, the Most Unmanly President," *Atlantic*, May
25, 2020, https://www.theatlantic.com/ideas/archive/2020/05/
donald-trump-the-most-unmanly-president/612031/.

5. And sure enough, three years later, and right on cue, Mark
Cuban appeared on Hannity during the coronavirus pandemic
and criticized Trump's (non)leadership in precisely these terms:
"You've got to be the strongest man in the game," Cuban said,
"but he's not"; John Haltiwanger, "Mark Cuban Rips Trump
during Interview with Sean Hannity: 'He Always Plays the Victim
Card,'" *Business Insider*, May 21, 2020, https://www.businessinsider
.com/mark-cuban-tells-sean-hannity-trump-always-plays-the
-victim-2020-5.

5. The Members-Only President Goes to Alabama

1. "An autopsy report, which was obtained by the *Baltimore
Sun*'s Justin Fenton, found Gray likely received the injury when

the van suddenly decelerated"; German Lopez, "The Baltimore Protests over Freddie Gray's Death, Explained," *Vox*, August 18, 2016, https://www.vox.com/2016/7/27/18089352/freddie-gray -baltimore-riots-police-violence.

2. Chris McGreal, "Anger as Local Police Union Chief Calls George Floyd a 'Violent Criminal,'" *Guardian*, June 1, 2020, https://www.theguardian.com/us-news/2020/jun/01/bob-kroll -george-floyd-minneapolis-police-union-chief.

3. *Race and Terror*, VICE documentary, HBO, at https://www .youtube.com/watch?v=RIrcB1sAN8I; BBC, "Charlottesville: Who Was Victim Heather Heyer?," August 14, 2017, https://www .bbc.com/news/world-us-canada-40924922.

4. Jeff Wiltse, interviewed by Rachel Martin, "Racial History of American Swimming Pools," *NPR*, May 6, 2008, https:// www.npr.org/templates/story/story.php?storyId=90213675. See also Wiltse, *Contested Waters: A Social History of Swimming Pools in America* (Chapel Hill: University of North Carolina Press, 2007).

5. A year and half later, during the coronavirus pandemic, Trump made the same pledge, in the same vein: "I will protect you if your governor fails," Trump said during his daily Covid-19 briefing from the White House before announcing his request that lawmakers refill the Paycheck Protection Program, to which Congress initially allocated $349 billion, after demand raided the account as businesses reeled from the pandemic outbreak. "Some governors fail. But when they fail, I will help"; John T. Bennett, "'I Will Protect You If Your Governor Fails': Trump Hails His 'Good Moves' in Coronavirus Fight," *Independent*, April 8, 2020, https://www.independent.co.uk/news/world/ americas/us-politics/trump-coronavirus-covid-19-governors -ventilators-who-a9454061.html.

6. An Empire unto Himself? Harvey Weinstein's Downfall

1. *Untouchable*, HULU, directed by, Ursula Macfarlane, 2019.

7. Race and the Revolving Door of (Un)Reality TV

1. *VEEP*, "Judge," directed by Beth McCarthy-Miller, written by Ted Cohen, HBO, June 11, 2017.

2. Jessica Goldstein, "*Veep* Recap: A Vortex of Sexual Confusion," *Vulture*, June 11, 2017, https://www.vulture.com/2017/06/veep-recap-season-6-episode-8.html.

3. Yamiche Alcindor, "Rep. Frederica Wilson on Trump: 'That Is Not What You Say to a Grieving Widow,'" *New York Times*, October 18, 2017, https://www.nytimes.com/2017/10/18/us/politics/congresswoman-wilson-trump-niger-call-widow.html.

4. Eugene Scott, "Accusations of Racism and Grandstanding Fly between Wilson and Kelly, Overtaking Big Questions about Niger Attack," *Washington Post*, October 20, 2017, https://www.washingtonpost.com/news/the-fix/wp/2017/10/20/accusations-of-racism-and-grandstanding-fly-between-wilson-and-kelly-overtaking-big-questions-about-niger-attack/.

5. Jeremy Diamond, "Kelly Erroneously Claimed Congresswoman Took Credit for Building Funding, Video Shows," *CNN*, October 20, 2017, https://www.cnn.com/2017/10/20/politics/frederica-wilson-john-kelly-video/index.html. On the video, Sophie Tatum, "Kelly Says He'll 'Never' Apologize for Comments about Rep. Frederica Wilson," *CNN*, October 31, 2017, https://www.cnn.com/2017/10/30/politics/john-kelly-frederica-wilson-apologize/index.html. Also, "Kelly did not dispute Wilson's account of the call, but instead indicated he advised Trump to say the words for which he is now drawing criticism, though Trump had previously said Wilson's account was 'totally fabricated'"; Diamond, "Kelly Calls Rep. Wilson an Empty Barrel in Recollection of 2015 FBI Ceremony," *CNN*, October 19, 2017, https://www.cnn.com/2017/10/19/politics/john-kelly-frederica-wilson-fbi/index.html. A year later, "Frederica Wilson says she never received an apology from outgoing White House chief of staff John Kelly after he falsely attacked her. Instead, she's received death threats and nooses in the mail over the past year"; Alex Daugherty, "Frederica Wilson Never Got an Apology from John Kelly. She got Nooses from Critics," *Miami Herald*, December 10, 2018, https://www.miamiherald.com/news/politics-government/article222899605.html.

8. They Want Civility, Let's Give It to Them

1. See also Gloria Borger, "Republicans Try a New Excuse to Defend Trump: It's Just a Joke," *CNN*, October 7, 2019, https://www.cnn.com/2019/10/07/politics/donald-trump-joking-gloria-borger/index.html, and Jennifer Mercieca, "When Trump Says He Was Being 'Sarcastic,' It's Just Part of His Gaslighting," *Washington Post*, April 25, 2020, https://www.washingtonpost.com/outlook/2020/04/25/when-trump-says-he-was-being-sarcastic-its-just-part-his-gaslighting/.

2. Anthony Bourdain, *Kitchen Confidential: Adventures in the Culinary Underbelly* (New York: Ecco, 2000).

3. Avi Selk and Sarah Murray, "The Owner of the Red Hen Explains Why She Asked Sarah Huckabee Sanders to Leave," *Washington Post*, June 25, 2018, https://www.washingtonpost.com/news/local/wp/2018/06/23/why-a-small-town-restaurant-owner-asked-sarah-huckabee-sanders-to-leave-and-would-do-it-again/.

4. Aaron Rupar, "Trump Seems to Think There'd Be No Coronavirus If There Was No Testing. It Doesn't Work Like That," *Vox*, May 15, 2020, https://www.vox.com/2020/5/15/21259888/trump-coronavirus-testing-very-few-cases.

5. Khuê Pham and Abdul Bari Hakim, "Elin Ersson and Ismail K.—How an Activist Tried in Vain to Rescue an Asylum-Seeker," *Deutsche Welle*, January 31, 2019, https://p.dw.com/p/3CRgK.

6. Ibid.

7. "Many legal complaints were lodged against her, but they didn't come from Turkish Airlines or the airport operator, as one might expect. Rather, they came from private citizens." Some were "people who had watched or read about the video." Others came from people on the plane. "Her actions caused a lot of confusion, irritation and worry inside the plane. Some of the passengers were quite upset about it," says prosecutor James von Reis. But, Ersson is unconcerned. "There has never been a case like this one, she explains, and says it's unclear if she committed a crime or not. 'Even if they do decide that I broke a law, I will probably only receive a fine of a few hundred euros,' she says." She is borne out; see Davis VanOpdorp, "Elin Ersson Sentenced

to Fine for Anti-Deportation Protest," *Deutsche Welle*, February 18, 2019, https://p.dw.com/p/3DYlg.

8. Pham and Hakim, "Elin Ersson and Ismail K.—How an Activist Tried in Vain to Rescue an Asylum-Seeker."

9. Ibid.

10. Selk and Murray, "The Owner of the Red Hen Explains Why She Asked Sarah Huckabee Sanders to Leave"; Sarah Huckabee Sanders, "Huckabee Sanders: Allowing Transgender People in the Military Is 'Expensive and Disruptive,'" *Washington Post*, July 26, 2017, video, 2:26, https://www.washingtonpost.com/video/national/huckabee-sanders-allowing-transgender-people-in-the-military-is-expensive-and-disruptive/2017/07/26/9c19cb54-7233-11e7-8c17-533c52b2f014_video.html. Erik Wemple, "'You're a Parent': Reporter Presses Sarah Huckabee Sanders on Immigration," *Washington Post*, June 14, 2018, https://www.washingtonpost.com/blogs/erik-wemple/wp/2018/06/14/youre-a-parent-reporter-presses-sarah-huckabee-sanders-on-immigration/.

9. Stormy Daniels's #MeToo Moment

1. Stormy Daniels, Interview by Anderson Cooper, "Stormy Daniels Describes Her Alleged Affair with Donald Trump," *60 Minutes*, CBS News, August 22, 2018, https://www.cbsnews.com/news/stormy-daniels-describes-her-alleged-affair-with-donald-trump-60-minutes-interview/.

2. Mary Trump's book came out as this one went to press, but it is noteworthy that she was called "honeybunch," too, by her Uncle Donald; Mary Trump, *Too Much and Never Enough* (New York: Simon and Schuster, 2020).

3. Alyssa Rosenberg, "The Most Radical Part of Anderson Cooper's Interview with Stormy Daniels," *Washington Post*, March 25, 2018, https://www.washingtonpost.com/news/act-four/wp/2018/03/25/the-most-radical-part-of-anderson-coopers-interview-with-stormy-daniels/.

10. The Trump Doctrine

1. Jane Coaston, "The White House Had to Protect Rob Porter to Save Donald Trump," *Vox*, February 9, 2018, https://www.vox

.com/policy-and-politics/2018/2/9/16994784/rob-porter-donald
-trump-john-kelly-white-house.

2. Jessica Winter, "The Language of the Trump
Administration Is the Language of Domestic Violence," *New
Yorker,* June 11, 2018, https://www.newyorker.com/culture/
cultural-comment/the-language-of-the-trump-administration
-is-the-language-of-domestic-violence.

3. Leah McElrath, Twitter post, June 2018, 12:56 p.m., https://
twitter.com/leahmcelrath/.

4. Kendra Lubalin, "America Is Literally in an Abusive
Relationship with Donald Trump," *Establishment,* September 29,
2016, https://medium.com/the-establishment/america-is-literally
-in-an-abusive-relationship-with-donald-trump-f862fc1e1fcc.

5. Quint Forgey, "Trump: DNC 'Should Be Ashamed' for
Russian Hack," *Politico,* July 15, 2018, https://www.politico.com/
story/2018/07/15/trump-russia-hack-democrats-dnc-722228.

6. Lubalin, "America Is Literally in an Abusive Relationship
with Donald Trump."

7. Niccolò Machiavelli, *The Prince,* trans. Tim Parks (London:
Penguin, 2009).

8. Nellie Bowles, "Thermostats, Locks and Lights: Digital
Tools of Domestic Abuse," *New York Times,* June 23, 2018, https://
www.nytimes.com/2018/06/23/technology/smart-home-devices
-domestic-abuse.html.

9. Ibid.

10. Machiavelli, *Prince.*

11. The default of belief does not mean we never doubt women.
It means belief is the starting point, from which we move to then
think and evaluate. So it does not mean that we *believe all women.*
As Susan Faludi points out, based on tracking its origins and
frequency in social media, the mantra that requires that we
"believe *all* women" is a right-wing talking point, used mostly not
by members of the #MeToo movement but by its detractors. Why?
Because, as Faludi explains, "the right knows what #MeToo
activists do well to keep in mind: Peril lies in purity. If the
pluralism of the women's movement can be reduced to rigid
boilerplate in the public mind, then the future of #MeToo will
have more to lose from a single untruthful woman whom it's

sworn to defend than from boatloads of predatory men." You can see the peril in Kelly Anne Conway's claim regarding later discredited #MeToo-type charges against Joe Biden: "Three magic words, 'Believe All Women.' I didn't hear an asterisk; I didn't see a footnote, 'Believe All Women so long as they are attacking somebody aligned with President Trump, Believe All Women so long as they are—have a college degree or better or are—are for abortion in the ninth month.'" As Faludi points out, however, "'Believe All Women' does have an asterisk: *It's never been feminist 'boilerplate.'" It is instead the worst kind of gaslighting; it takes our words for its purposes, alters them ever so slightly and deniably, and then uses them against us; Susan Faludi, "'Believe All Women' Is a Right-Wing Trap," *New York Times*, May 18, 2020, https://www.nytimes.com/2020/05/18/opinion/tara-reade-believe-all-women.html.

11. Jon Stewart and the Limits of Mockery

1. *The China Syndrome* is the name of a 1979 film about a nuclear meltdown. See also *Chinatown*, directed by Roman Polanski, written by Robert Towne (Paramount, 1974).

2. A year later, Wiesel was awarded the 1986 Nobel Peace Prize for being "one of the most important spiritual leaders and guides in an age when violence, repression, and racism continue to characterize the world" (Wiesel was an agnostic). In his acceptance speech Wiesel said, "Silence encourages the tormentor, never the tormented. Sometimes we must interfere. When human lives are endangered, when human dignity is in jeopardy, national borders and sensitivities become irrelevant"; *Wikipedia, The Free Encyclopedia*, s.v. "Elie Wiesel," accessed June 19, 2020, https://en.wikipedia.org/wiki/Elie_Wiesel.

3. "Ronald Reagan was offered the support of the Klan in both 1980 and 1984. 'I have no tolerance whatsoever for what the Klan represents,' he said in 1980 after a meeting with Jesse Jackson. 'Indeed, I resent them using my name'"; Philip Bump, "For Decades, the Ku Klux Klan Openly Endorsed Candidates for Political Office," *Washington Post*, February 29, 2016,

https://www.washingtonpost.com/news/the-fix/wp/2016/02/29/
for-decades-the-ku-klux-klan-openly-endorsed-candidates-for
-political-office/?utm_term=.27dbb68dab92. Four years later,
the KKK endorsed him again, and Reagan repudiated the
endorsement, though he arguably had sought it by first declaring
his candidacy in Mississippi. "The politics of racial hatred and
religious bigotry practiced by the Klan and others have no place
in this country, and are destructive of the values for which
America has always stood," he said in a letter. "A White House
spokesman, Anson Frank, said that the president signed the letter
while in China and that it was delivered today to Morris B.
Abram, a Civil Rights Commission member who requested it
after reading news reports that Klan leaders in Georgia had
endorsed Mr. Reagan. When the Klan endorsement was first
reported last month, neither the White House nor the president's
reelection campaign committee would comment on it. In
his letter to Mr. Abram, the president said, 'While in China, I
have been distressed to learn that some individuals back home
have questioned whether my views on the Ku Klux Klan have
somehow changed since 1980. Nothing could be further from
the truth'"; UPI, "Reagan Spurns Klan Support," *New York
Times*, May 2, 1984, https://www.nytimes.com/1984/05/02/us/
reagan-spurns-klan-support.html.

4. Jon Stewart, "Jon Stewart Is Ready to Negotiate with
Donald Trump," *The Late Show with Stephen Colbert*, June 28,
2018, video, 7:51, https://www.cbs.com/shows/the-late-show-with
-stephen-colbert/video/rZuRc6hvPHNDgUakcS6gAeg7UQ
_wVRJ3/jon-stewart-is-ready-to-negotiate-with-donald-trump/.

5. See Nicole Hemmer, "It's Always Been Hard to Say No to
Citizenship Requests from Soldiers. Trump's Doing It," *Vox*,
July 9, 2018, https://www.vox.com/the-big-idea/2018/7/9/17549402/
citizenship-military-mavni-immigration-service-naturalization
-discharge-history-mavni, and Ailsa Chang, "White House
Launches Effort to Take Citizenship from Those Who Lied to
Get It," *NPR*, July 4, 2018, https://www.npr.org/2018/07/04/
625980910/white-house-launches-effort-to-take-citizenship-from
-those-who-lied-to-get-it. Indeed, in an irony that historians may

later remark, it was at this very moment that the U.S. Supreme Court finally renounced the *Korematsu* decision, not, however, to render problematic the new tent cities in Texas then going up to warehouse migrants and asylum-seekers, but to disavow any analogy to Trump's Muslim ban and thus to allow, in their decision on that case, executive prejudice to become, once again, policy without judicial intervention; Josh Gerstein, "Supreme Court Repudiates Infamous Korematsu Ruling," *Politico*, June 26, 2018, https://www.politico.com/story/2018/06/26/supreme -court-overturns-korematsu-673846.

6. Although he has offered up Dickens, in the end Stewart seems to say that even that reference is too high culture for this clown. Paradoxically, mocking Trump as a clown also risks elevating him to world-historical significance, however. That is precisely how Charlie Chaplin responded to Hitler in his time: by mocking the dictator as a clown and buffoon. Chaplin played the same game as Stewart. Lampooning his own masculinity, he anticipated Stewart's effeminate talk with his own effeminate walk and let others think he was hiding his Jewishness. (Chaplin was not Jewish but when asked about it he would refuse to answer, since that would breach solidarity with those at that moment threatened with genocide.)

12. Bullying Canada: An American Presidential Tradition

1. Dan Bilefsky and Catherine Porter, "Trump's 'Bully' Attack on Trudeau Outrages Canadians," *New York Times*, June 10, 2018, https://www.nytimes.com/2018/06/10/world/canada/g-7-justin -trudeau-trump.html.

2. "Locations," *Betty Ford Center*, accessed June 20, 2020, https://www.hazeldenbettyford.org/locations/betty-ford-center -rancho-mirage.

3. Lawrence Martin, "In Election Campaign Collusion, JFK and Lester Pearson Showed the Way," *Globe and Mail*, May 22, 2018, https://www.theglobeandmail.com/opinion/article-in -election-campaign-collusion-jfk-and-lester-pearson-showed -the-way/.

4. Joseph A. Esposito, *Dinner in Camelot: The Night America's Greatest Scientists, Writers, and Scholars Partied at the Kennedy White House* (Lebanon, N.H.: ForeEdge, 2018).

5. Mark Feldstein, *Poisoning the Press: Richard Nixon, Jack Anderson, and the Rise of Washington's Scandal Culture* (New York: Farrar, Straus and Giroux, 2010).

6. Janet DiGiacomo, "Woman Who Accused Justin Trudeau of Groping Breaks Her Silence," *CNN*, July 7, 2018, https://edition.cnn.com/2018/07/06/americas/justin-trudeau-groping-allegations/index.html.

7. Scott Neuman, "Canada's Justin Trudeau Rejects Coalition in Favor of Minority Government," *NPR*, October 24, 2019, https://www.npr.org/2019/10/24/772945398/canadas-trudeau-rejects-coalition-in-favor-of-minority-government.

8. Josh K. Elliott, "Why Trudeau Has Become Trump's Newest Twitter Target," *Global News*, June 11, 2018, https://globalnews.ca/news/4266285/canada-us-donald-trump-justin-trudeau-twitter-attack-g7/.

9. See Chapter 4.

10. By 2020 the Lincoln Project formed, and its efforts in the run-up to the 2020 election are invaluable to those seeking to break the grip of Trumpism. That said, no recovery will be possible without confronting, and not just disavowing, the deep *continuities* between the Republican party's operations in the twentieth century and since and Trump's racism, misogyny, plunder of the public purse, and more.

11. Anonymous, "I Am Part of the Resistance Inside the Trump Administration," *New York Times*, September 5, 2018, https://www.nytimes.com/2018/09/05/opinion/trump-white-house-anonymous-resistance.html.

13. House Renovations: For Christine Blasey Ford

1. On the constraints, the failure to return calls from witnesses, and so on, see Jackie Calmes, "New Reporting Details How FBI Limited Investigation of Kavanaugh Allegations," *Los Angeles Times*, September 16, 2019, https://www.latimes.com/politics/story/2019-09-16/fbi-investigation-brett-kavanaugh-confirmation.

2. There were others, too, like Amy Klobuchar and Kamala Harris, who work there and asked the questions that skillfully revealed the bully that Kavanaugh denied he ever was; Molly Hensley-Clark, "Kamala Harris and Amy Klobuchar, Both Former Prosecutors, Stood Out in the Brett Kavanaugh Hearings," *Buzzfeed News*, September 17, 2018, https://www.buzzfeednews.com/article/mollyhensleyclancy/kamala-harris-brett-kavanaugh-amy-klobuchar-hearings-senate.

14. No Collision: Opting Out of Catastrophe

1. "Fourth National Climate Assessment," *The National Climate Assessment*, accessed June 18, 2020, https://nca2018.globalchange.gov/.

2. Hilary Brueck, "President Trump Said His Uncle Was a 'Great Professor at MIT for Many Years'—Here's What to Know about John Trump," *Business Insider*, October 17, 2018, https://www.businessinsider.com/donald-trump-uncle-john-trump-mit-nuclear-scientist-2018-10. In March 2020, he was saying exactly the same thing regarding his ability to deal with the coronavirus contagion, that he had a "knack" for science, that everyone says so, and that it might be his genes, given his uncle John had been at MIT; David Nakamura, "'Maybe I Have a Natural Ability': Trump Plays Medical Expert on Coronavirus by Second-Guessing the Professionals," *Washington Post*, March 7, 2020, https://www.washingtonpost.com/politics/maybe-i-have-a-natural-ability-trump-plays-medical-expert-on-coronavirus-by-second-guessing-the-professionals/2020/03/06/3ee0574c-5ffb-11ea-9055-5fa12981bbbf_story.html.

3. *Melancholia*, directed by Lars Von Trier (Magnolia Pictures, 2011), DVD. I discuss the film in greater detail in Bonnie Honig, *Public Things: Democracy in Disrepair* (New York: Fordham University Press, 2017).

4. "Home," *Rising S Company*, accessed June 20, 2020, https://risingsbunkers.com/.

5. Olivia Carville, "The Super Rich of Silicon Valley Have a Doomsday Escape Plan," *Bloomberg*, September 5, 2018, https://

www.bloomberg.com/features/2018-rich-new-zealand-doomsday
-preppers/.

6. Alyson Krueger, "Climate Change Insurance: Buy Land Somewhere Else," *New York Times*, November 30, 2018, https://www.nytimes.com/2018/11/30/realestate/climate-change-insurance-buy-land-somewhere-else.html.

7. Kate Andersen Brower, "Former White House Residence Staff Appalled by Donald Trump's 'Real Dump' Comment," *Time*, August 2, 2017, https://time.com/4884923/white-house-donald-trump-dump/.

8. Elaine Scarry, *Thinking in an Emergency* (New York: W. W. Norton, 2011).

9. Ibid.

10. Carville, "Super Rich of Silicon Valley Have a Doomsday Escape Plan."

11. Hugh Hunt, "Blocking Out the Sun Won't Fix Climate Change—But It Could Buy Us Time," *Conversation*, November 19, 2015, https://theconversation.com/blocking-out-the-sun-wont-fix-climate-change-but-it-could-buy-us-time-50818.

12. Audre Lorde, *Sister Outsider* (Berkeley, Calif.: Crossing Press, 2007), 38.

13. Hunt, "Blocking Out the Sun Won't Fix Climate Change—But It Could Buy Us Time"; Herman Melville, *Moby-Dick; or, The Whale* (New York: W. W. Norton, 2002), 140.

14. Krueger, "Climate Change Insurance: Buy Land Somewhere Else."

15. Robinson Meyer, "The Democratic Party Wants to Make Climate Policy Exciting," *Atlantic*, December 5, 2018, https://www.theatlantic.com/science/archive/2018/12/ocasio-cortez-green-new-deal-winning-climate-strategy/576514/.

16. As Ruthie Gilmore puts it, "For people trying to solve their everyday problems, behaving in a violent and life-annihilating way is not a solution"; Rachel Kushner, "Is Prison Necessary? Ruth Wilson Gilmore Might Change Your Mind," *New York Times*, April 17, 2019, https://www.nytimes.com/2019/04/17/magazine/prison-abolition-ruth-wilson-gilmore.html.

17. W. E. B. Du Bois's short story "The Comet," also about the end of the world, suggests he may have entertained similar

thoughts, about ending the world of the undeserving with a catastrophe neither deserved nor undeserved, as random as the skin color invested with so much meaning in the U.S.; Du Bois, *Darkwater: Voices from Within the Veil* (New York: Verso, 2016).

18. Krueger, "Climate Change Insurance: Buy Land Somewhere Else."

15. Epstein, Barr, and the Virus of Civic Fatigue (with Sara Rushing)

1. The original post on which this is based was coauthored with Sara Rushing. For this volume, I made a few small changes and updates, with my coauthor's consent.

2. Adam Ramsay, "Boris Johnson Made Politics Awful, Then Asked People to Vote It Away," *Open Democracy*, December 22, 2019, https://www.opendemocracy.net/en/opendemocracyuk/boris-johnson-made-politics-awful-then-asked-people-vote-it-away/.

16. Mueller, They Wrote

1. James Poniewozik, "Asked to Put on a Show, Mueller Wishes You'd Read the Book," *New York Times*, July 24, 2019, https://www.nytimes.com/2019/07/24/arts/television/mueller-testimony-trump.html.

2. Robert Mueller, "Robert Mueller Testifies Before Congress," C-SPAN, July 24, 2019, YouTube video, 7:34:08, https://youtu.be/6b_EuIJhgOk.

3. Jen Kirby, "Mueller Defends His Team against Republican Attacks of Political Bias," *Vox*, July 24, 2019, https://www.vox.com/2019/7/24/20708653/mueller-testimony-defends-integrity-political-bias-witch-hunt.

17. *Unbelievable*: Scenes from a Structure

1. *Unbelievable*, created by Susannah Grant, Ayelet Waldman, and Michael Chabon (CBS Television Studios, 2019), Netflix.

2. Sophie Gilbert, *"Unbelievable* Is TV's Most Humane Show,"
Atlantic, September 19, 2019, https://www.theatlantic.com/
entertainment/archive/2019/09/netflix-unbelievable-sexual-assault
-revolutionary-competence/598411/.

3. W. E. B. Du Bois, *The Souls of Black Folk* (New York: W. W.
Norton, 1999).

4. Pamela Karlan belongs on this list, as well. When she
appeared as part of the House impeachment hearings, she
responded to Republican congressman Dough Collins's dismissal
in advance of her testimony, suggesting she had not had time to
read everything or know what was going on, with this: "Here
Mr. Collins I would like to say to you, sir, that I read transcripts
of every one of the witnesses who appeared in the live hearing
because I would not speak about these things without reviewing
the facts," she said. "So I'm insulted by the suggestion that as a
law professor I don't care about those facts"; Aaron Rupar,
"Impeachment Hearings: Law Professor Pamela Karlan Had No
Patience for Rep. Doug Collins's insults," *Vox*, December 4, 2019,
https://www.vox.com/2019/12/4/20995296/pamela-karlan-doug
-collins-impeachment-hearing-house-judiciary.

18. Gothic Girls: *Bombshell*'s Variation on a Theme

1. In my 2001 book *Democracy and the Foreigner*, I singled
out female gothics as the genre of democracy; Bonnie Honig,
Democracy and the Foreigner (Princeton, N.J.: Princeton
University Press, 2001). Others have since taken up the idea,
most recently Shindo Reiko, "Untranslatable Community:
Toward a Gothic Way of Speaking," in *Belonging in Translation:
Solidarity and Migrant Activism in Japan* (Bristol: Bristol
University Press, 2019).

2. They combine the best of paranoia (always questioning,
taking notes, making observations, keeping records, which helps
when you need to escape the clutches of rotten men or corrupt
political leaders) with repair (making new connections that
nourish and support one another's efforts to regain one's balance,
heal from the past, and build a future). Rachel Maddow, who has

certainly followed a practice of paranoid reading for the last four years, has been lampooned as a conspiracy theorist peddling paranoia to liberals who see conspiracy everywhere. And there have been moments that look a lot like that. But with the Lev Parnas revelations of January 2020, it certainly seems likelier that she has, like a lot of gothic heroines, been onto something important as a result of reading practices that are healthily diligent, determinedly empirical, and properly distrustful. On this, see the recent work of Noga Rotem, who argues that there is actually something reparative *in* paranoia itself; Rotem, "Paranoid and Reparative Politics from Arendt to Hobbes" (PhD diss., Brown University, 2020).

3. That is why, in *Gaslight* and other examples of the conventional gothic genre, the women are often maternalized (as we saw in Chapter 2) and the men castrated. That is the misogyny of gothics, which require a counter-reading if they are to be of use to democratic theory and feminist criticism. See *Gaslight*, directed by George Cukor (MGM, 1944), DVD.

4. *Bombshell*, directed by Jay Roach (Lionsgate, 2019), DVD. The female gothic formula is given a great twist in *Get Out* (dir. Jordan Peele, Universal, 2017), in which the conventional gender roles are reversed and the gaslighting that is the genre's characteristic feature is not because of one bad man's greed or lasciviousness, but a feature of the reality-dominating white supremacy that operates only semi-secretly and with impunity.

5. Nick Allen, "Who's Who in *Bombshell*: A Character Guide," *Vulture*, January 3, 2020, https://www.vulture.com/2020/01/bombshell-cast-of-characters-and-true-story-behind-each.html.

6. Notably, the actress Margot Robbie said that, "during character development, she mapped out Kayla['s] entire career into her 60s," which is precisely what the film does for her (ibid.). *Bombshell* also features Kate McKinnon as a character (also a composite) held captive, in effect the proverbial princess in the tower who will never succumb and never escape. Her conscience is kept alive by photographs: one of herself with a girlfriend moves on and off her desk, and another, a poster of Hillary Clinton, hangs in her bathroom.

19. Boxed In: Debbie Dingell vs. Donald Trump

1. Donald J. Trump, Twitter post, December 2017, 8:03 a.m., https://twitter.com/realDonaldTrump/.

2. Josh Gerstein, "Rod Rosenstein Says He Made Call to Release Strzok-Page Texts," *Politico*, January 18, 2020, https://www.politico.com/news/2020/01/18/rosenstein-strzok-page-texts-100776.

3. Thanks to Jeff Tulis on these points. Kathleen Gray, "Donald Trump Takes Shot at U.S. Rep. Debbie Dingell, Her Husband John Dingell at rally," *USA Today*, December 19, 2019, https://www.usatoday.com/story/news/politics/2019/12/19/donald-trump-bashes-debbie-dingell-john-dingell-battle-creek-rally/2696014001/.

4. Chris Cillizza, "Donald Trump's Disgusting and Deplorable Attack on Debbie Dingell," *CNN*, December 19, 2019, https://www.cnn.com/2019/12/19/politics/donald-trump-debbie-dingell-john-dingell/index.html.

5. Emma Donoghue, *Room* (New York: Little, Brown, 2010).

6. John Bowden, "Trump Clashes with Reporter during Coronavirus Briefing: 'Be Nice,'" *The Hill*, March 29, 2020, https://thehill.com/homenews/administration/490093-trump-gets-in-back-and-forth-with-reporter-during-coronavirus.

20. Mediating Masculinity: Rambo Republicanism and the Long Iran Crisis

1. Matthew Weaver, "Trump Says Iran Will Never Have a Nuclear Weapon as Tehran Mourns Suleimani—As It Happened," *Guardian*, January 6, 2020, https://www.theguardian.com/world/live/2020/jan/06/iran-qassem-suleimani-funeral-donald-trump-nato-iraq.

2. Donald J. Trump, Twitter post, January 2020, 5:52 p.m., https://twitter.com/realDonaldTrump/.

3. Noting that the B-52 is a "Cold War–era bomber," Oriana Pawlyk reported on Military.com that the "U.S. Air Force is sending six B-52 Stratofortress bombers to Diego Garcia, a military hub that acts as a strategic location for operations in

both the Middle East and the Pacific"; Pawlyk, "Air Force Sends B-52 Bombers to Diego Garcia Amid Middle East Buildup: Report," *Military.com*, January 6, 2020, https://www.military.com/daily-news/2020/01/06/air-force-sends-b-52-bombers-diego-garcia-amid-middle-east-buildup-report.html.

4. *Dictionary.com*, s.v. "House of Cards," accessed June 20, 2020, https://www.dictionary.com/browse/house-of-cards.

5. *Rambo: First Blood Part II*, directed by George P. Cosmatos (TriStar Pictures, 1985), DVD.

6. Poppy Noor, "Trump Posted a Picture of Himself as Rocky. No One Knows What to Make of It," *Guardian*, November 27, 2019, https://www.theguardian.com/us-news/2019/nov/27/donald-trump-rocky-picture-twitter.

7. Scout Tafoya, "Film Review: Rambo; Last Blood Is a Republican Wet Dream," *Consequence of Sound*, September 21, 2019, https://consequenceofsound.net/2019/09/film-review-rambo-last-blood/.

8. Simon Abrams, "Sylvester Stallone's Rambo Has Devolved into a Hyperbolic Symbol of Right-Wing Politics," *Esquire*, September 23, 2019, https://www.esquire.com/entertainment/movies/a29189408/sylvester-stallone-rambo-right-wing-politics-symbol/.

9. Matt Taibbi, "Donald Trump Claims Authorship of Legendary Reagan Slogan; Has Never Heard of Google," *Rolling Stone*, March 25, 2015, https://www.rollingstone.com/politics/politics-news/donald-trump-claims-authorship-of-legendary-reagan-slogan-has-never-heard-of-google-193834/.

10 Donald J. Trump, "Trump Ridicules Bush's 'Thousand Points of Light,'" *Washington Post*, July 6, 2018, video, 0:43, https://www.washingtonpost.com/video/politics/other/trump-ridicules-bushs-thousand-points-of-light/2018/07/06/faecd4f2-8135-11e8-b3b5-b61896f90919_video.html.

11. Michael D'Antonio, "When Donald Trump Hated Ronald Reagan," *Politico*, October 25, 2015, https://www.politico.com/magazine/story/2015/10/donald-trump-ronald-reagan-213288.

12. Charles P. Pierce, "It Is Impossible Now for the United States and Iran to Disentangle Themselves," *Esquire*, 2018,

https://link.esquire.com/view/5bf578b024c17c5aa31df568bclto
.4nq/d2aabdf2.

13. Gary Sick, *October Surprise: America's Hostages in Iran
and the Election of Ronald Reagan* (New York: Time, 1991).
"Investigating the October Surprise," PBS Frontline, Season
1992: Episode 16. See also Walter Pincus, "'October Surprise'
Story Unfounded, Report Says," *Washington Post*, November 24,
1992, at https://www.washingtonpost.com/archive/politics/1992/11/
24/october-surprise-story-unfounded-report-says/2c0ed858-f45c
-4f79-98a1-86e626330a54/.

14. As is Facebook, too; Nick Corasaniti, "Days after
Suleimani Killing, Trump Campaign Promotes It on Facebook,"
New York Times, January 7, 2020, https://www.nytimes.com/2020/
01/07/us/politics/trump-facebook-ads-iran.html.

15. Rebecca Davis, "Cannes: Sylvester Stallone Says 'Rambo'
Wasn't 'Meant to Be a Political Statement,'" *Variety*, May 24,
2019, https://variety.com/2019/film/news/cannes-sylvester-stallone
-rocky-rambo-political-1203225438/.

16. Ashley Parker and Philip Rucker, "How Trump's Attempts
to Win the Daily News Cycle Feed a Chaotic Coronavirus
Response," *Washington Post*, April 4, 2020, https://www
.washingtonpost.com/politics/trump-daily-reality-show-corona
virus-response/2020/04/04/97932e34-75c5-11ea-87da-77a8136
c1a6d_story.html.

17. Lawrence Glickman, Twitter post, April 2020, 9:15 a.m.,
https://twitter.com/LarryGlickman.

18. Martin Pengelly, "Donald Trump Jr. and Ivanka Trump
among Top Republican Picks for 2024," *Guardian*, January 4,
2020, https://www.theguardian.com/us-news/2020/jan/04/
donald-trump-jr-ivanka-trump-2024-presidential-election-poll.

19. Heather Cox Richardson, "April 4, 2020," *Letter from an
American*, April 5, 2020, https://heathercoxrichardson.substack
.com/p/april-4-2020.

21. "13 Angry Democrats"? A Noir Reading of *12 Angry Men*

1. After Mueller testified before the House in July 2019, it
was 18 angry Democrats. *New York Times*: "He complained

again about the '18 angry Democrats' he asserted were on the Mueller team and asked why the special counsel did not investigate 'Lyin' & Leakin' James Comey,' the former F.B.I. director whom Mr. Trump fired, and others"; Shear and Fadulu, "Trump Says Mueller Was 'Horrible' and Republicans 'Had a Good Day.'"

2. *12 Angry Men*, directed by Sidney Lumet (United Artists, 1957).

3. William E. Connolly, "The Ethos of Sovereignty," in *Law and the Sacred*, ed. Austin Sarat et al. (Stanford, Calif.: Stanford University Press, 2007).

4. On the hypermasculinity of Trump supporters, see Connolly, *Aspirational Fascism: The Struggle for Multifaceted Democracy under Trump* (Minneapolis: University of Minnesota Press, 2017).

5. James Sterngold, "A Tense Jury Room Revisited, And Racism Is Given a Twist," *New York Times*, August 17, 1997, https://www.nytimes.com/1997/08/17/arts/a-tense-jury-room-revisited-and-racism-is-given-a-twist.html.

6. Recall the similar message, telegraphed in *Bombshell*. (directed by Jay Roach, written by Charles Randolph [Lionsgate, 2019]). After the evil ogre Roger Ailes has been toppled, the camera looks up to his announced replacement or placeholder: Bill Shine, who was "never accused of harassment himself. But . . . was accused in lawsuits of turning a blind eye to a climate that was hostile toward women." On July 5, 2018, Shine was named White House deputy chief of staff for communications and months later was transferred to work on the 2020 campaign. There is more than one castle in our gothic story and more than one ogre; Maggie Haberman, "Bill Shine, Ousted from Fox News in Scandal, Joins White House Communications Team," *New York Times*, July 5, 2018, https://www.nytimes.com/2018/07/05/us/politics/bill-shine-white-house-communications.html.

22. In the Streets a Serenade: Siena under Lockdown

1. BBC, "Coronavirus: English Local Elections Postponed for a Year," March 13, 2020, https://www.bbc.com/news/uk-politics-51876269.

2. Trump constantly criticizes mail-in voting, though he himself uses it. He claims with no basis that it is ripe for corruption. There is no evidence for this at all. I mention in an earlier essay in this volume his attacks on Michigan's attorney general in May 2020, which was for mailing out to Michigan residents applications for vote-by-mail ballots. And in Chapter 25, "Impenetrable: Gaslighting the 14th Amendment," I look at what Trump is doing when he targets voting as a Democratic plot. In a new development, as of May 27, 2020, Twitter has flagged these tirades as misleading and connected Twitter users through them to accurate voting information.

23. Isn't It Ironic? Spitballing in a Pandemic

1. Kenneth P. Vogel, "Trump Nominee Draws Scrutiny for Ties to Ukrainian Energy Interests," *New York Times*, October 10, 2018, https://www.nytimes.com/2018/10/10/us/politics/william -bryan-homeland-security.html. See also Daniel Funke, "In Context: What Donald Trump Said about Disinfectant, Sun and Coronavirus," *Politifact*, April 24, 2020, https://www.politifact .com/article/2020/apr/24/context-what-donald-trump-said-about -disinfectant-/.

2. Donald J. Trump, "Trump on Coronavirus: 'People Are Really Surprised I Understand This Stuff,'" *BBC*, March 9, 2020, video, 1:32, https://www.bbc.com/news/av/world-us-canada -51761880/trump-on-coronavirus-people-are-really-surprised-i -understand-this-stuff/.

3. "Epstein avoided major punishment for his crimes, due to a deal his lawyers worked out with the then-district attorney in Miami, Alexander Acosta. Acosta is now President Trump's labor secretary, and he oversees agencies charged with stopping human trafficking"; Julie Brown, "How Jeffrey Epstein Avoided a Life Sentence in Prison," *NHPR*, 2018, https://www.nhpr.org/ post/how-jeffrey-epstein-avoided-life-sentence-prison#stream/o. Epstein pled guilty to two felony charges in state court. In exchange, he and his associates received immunity from federal sex-trafficking charges, and the investigation was sealed—

hiding Epstein's crimes from the view of the public and other victims.

4. Funke, "In Context: What Donald Trump Said about Disinfectant, Sun and Coronavirus."

5. Daniel W. Drezner, *The Toddler in Chief: What Donald Trump Teaches Us about the Modern Presidency* (Chicago: University of Chicago Press, 2020).

6. Reed Richardson, "WH Tried to Force CNN's Kaitlan Collins to Move to Back Row at Briefing, Reported Threatened Secret Service Involvement," *Mediaite*, April 24, 2020, https://www.mediaite.com/news/wh-tried-to-force-cnns-kaitlan-collins-to-move-to-back-row-at-briefing-reportedly-threatened-secret-service-involvement/.

7. Sheryl Gay Stolberg, "Virus Whistle-Blower Says Trump Administration Steered Contracts to Cronies," *New York Times*, May 5, 2020, https://www.nytimes.com/2020/05/05/us/politics/rick-bright-coronavirus-whistleblower.html.

24. Build That Wall: The Politics of Motherhood in Portland

1. This post draws on reporting by Sergio Olmos and Tuck Woodstock in Portland.

2. Stuart Schrader, "Trump Has Brought America's Dirty Wars Home," *The New Republic*, July 21, 2020.

3. "Naked Athena Speaks Out," *Elle*, https://www.elle.com/culture/career-politics/a33432833/naked-athena-speaks-out/.

25. Impenetrable: Gaslighting the 14th Amendment

1. In mid-May 2020, Trump "accused Democrats in California of attempting to 'steal another election' after it was revealed mail-in ballots will be sent to every registered voter in the state." This was an off-cycle election to replace Katy Hill, forced out of her House seat when nude photos of her were "leaked on a conservative website without her consent" and "authors of the original articles, which published these intimate photos, were former campaign advisors to Steve Knight, the former congressman whom Hill beat in her 2018 run for

Congress." In May 2020, Republicans regained the seat; Lauren Lantry, "Reflecting on her 2019 Scandal, Former Rep. Katie Hill Says She Still Hasn't 'Fully Recovered,'" *ABC News*, February 21, 2020, https://abcnews.go.com/Politics/reflecting -2019-photo-scandal-rep-katie-hill-fully/story?id=69105515.

2. Martha S. Jones, "The Real Origins of Birthright Citizenship," *Atlantic*, October 31, 2018, https://www.theatlantic .com/ideas/archive/2018/10/birthright-citizenship-was-won-freed -slaves/574498/. See also Jones, *Birthright Citizens: A History of Race and Rights in Antebellum America* (Cambridge: Cambridge University Press, 2018).

3. Is "bloodmixing" too strong? On May 21, 2020, Trump visited a Ford Motor Company plant and congratulated the company's original founder on his good bloodlines, thus taking off the mask in two ways. The state's attorney general, Dana Nessel, warned that masks are required in the plant (and threatened to sue the company if he did not wear one and to bar Trump from "any enclosed facilities inside our state. 'I think we're going to take action against any company or any facility that allows him inside those facilities and puts our workers at risk. We simply can't afford it here in our state,' she said"; Justin Vallejo, "Michigan Threatens to Sue Companies That Let Donald Trump Inside without a Mask," *Independent*, May 21, 2020, https://www.independent.co.uk/news/world/americas/us -politics/michigan-donald-trump-mask-attorney-general-dana -nessel-legal-action-ford-a9527411.html. Trump, who had thus far refused to wear one, put on a mask briefly during his visit, mostly off camera, but then took it off. When he spoke, now maskless, a second mask came off as he praised the "good bloodlines" of Henry Ford, "a notorious antisemite admired by Adolf Hitler, during a taxpayer-funded tour he treated like one of his aborted arena campaign rallies with supporters"; Joe Sommerlad and Justin Vallejo, "Trump News—Live: Drug Taken by President Linked to Increased Risk of Death, as Poll shows 60 Per Cent of Americans Disapprove of Coronavirus Response," *Independent*, May 22, 2020, https://www.independent.co.uk/news/world/ americas/us-politics/trump-news-live-coronavirus-press-briefing -white-house-twitter-us-update-latest-a9527786.html.

4. In *Gaslight*, Gregory accuses Paula of stealing his watch, which he himself has taken from her purse, where he earlier made a show of putting it for safekeeping. And he accuses her of desiring Brian Cameron, whom she does not know and, at that point, is hardly aware of.

5. Eliza Relman, "The 25 Women Who Have Accused Trump of Sexual Misconduct," *Business Insider*, May 1, 2020, https://www.businessinsider.com/women-accused-trump-sexual-misconduct-list-2017-12.

6. Since his election, Trump has defended many men credibly accused of sexual assault: Roy Moore, Bill O'Reilly, Roger Ailes, Robert Roger Porter, Brett Kavanaugh. Trump has no interest in assaults on women and does not hesitate to call misogynists and Nazis, too, for that matter, good people. So why is it that Trump raises a general policy worry that illegal immigration will bring criminals to the U.S., but then focuses mostly on this one particular kind of crime, and one particular kind of assault? I explain why in terms of a border anxiety that runs through American politics, as Michael Rogin and others have long pointed out. But, as Jeffrey Tulis reminds me, it is worth noting a further detail: Trump often projects his own vice onto the object of his enmity. In case the projection boomerangs back on to him, he reminds the listener that some rapists, like himself, are good people. Thus, he projects his vice and wraps himself in another's virtue. So, too, in his treatment of Joe Biden, who, Trump suggests, has sexually assaulted women and children, but whose perceived virtue—niceness—Trump appropriates for himself.

7. I discuss the book in detail in Bonnie Honig, *Democracy and the Foreigner* (Princeton, N.J.: Princeton University Press, 2001).

8. Sometimes these expulsions target other U.S. citizens, too. In other words, it is not just that some immigrants who attain citizenship are denationalized, or that so-called anchor babies are expelled, but also U.S. citizens. See the excellent work of Jacqueline Stevens at the States without Nations blog.

9. Michael Tackett and Michael Wines, "Trump Disbands Commission on Voter Fraud," *New York Times*, January 3, 2018, https://www.nytimes.com/2018/01/03/us/politics/trump-voter

-fraud-commission.html. In May 2020, Trump expanded his charges of illegal voting from illegals voting to illegal voting, targeting in particular voting by mail: "They send in thousands and thousands of fake ballots," as if mail-in voting is as such fraudulent. "It shouldn't be something where they send you a pile of stuff and you send it back," Trump said, charging that absentee ballots are prone to "massive manipulation"; Donald J. Trump, "Remarks by President Trump in a Meeting with Governor Hutchinson of Arkansas and Governor Kelly of Kansas," *White House*, May 20, 2020, https://www.whitehouse.gov/briefings -statements/remarks-president-trump-meeting-governor -hutchinson-arkansas-governor-kelly-kansas/.

10. Tackett and Wines, "Trump Disbands Commission on Voter Fraud." Importantly, the investigation referred to here happened under the second President Bush. That is, this is Republican Party politicking. In spite of there being no evidence of fraud, soon after becoming president, Trump put Kris Kobach in charge of a commission on voting fraud to provide evidence to back up his false claim. The commission was soon disbanded when it could not find any instances of fraud, citing states' refusal to provide the commission with voting rolls and citizenship data. Perhaps they should have looked in North Carolina, where the only genuine case of election-fraud was committed recently by Republicans, found guilty of ballot tampering; Richard Gonzales, "North Carolina GOP Operative Faces New Felony Charges That Allege Ballot Fraud," *NPR*, July 30, 2019, https://www.npr.org/2019/ 07/30/746800630/north-carolina-gop-operative-faces-new-felony -charges-that-allege-ballot-fraud.

11. Donald J. Trump, Twitter post, May 2020, 11:45 a.m., https://www.dailymail.co.uk/news/article-8303637/Trump-accuses -Democrats-trying-steal-election.html.

12. The real issue for those interested in actual election integrity has to do with the widespread use of voting machines, which are vulnerable to hacking and vote-switching. Experts argue that nothing is safer for election integrity than hand- marked paper ballots, which, as it happens, is a feature of mail-in voting to which Trump may also be opposed for this

very reason. See Jennifer Cohn, "How New Voting Machines Could Hack Our Democracy," *NYRB*, December 17, 2019, https://www.nybooks.com/daily/2019/12/17/how-new-voting -machines-could-hack-our-democracy/.

13. The Georgia story is worth reading about in its entirety; Carrie Teegardin, "Race and Politics at Issue in Case against Coffee County Official," *AJC*, March 15, 2018, https://www.ajc .com/blog/investigations/jury-quickly-says-not-guilty-georgia -elections-case/uxbnZO4AUxmBQfTmVGZjXK/. So is the Texas case, which is heartbreaking. Ironically, as many pointed out on Twitter, Trump himself likely cast an illegal ballot in the 2020 Florida Republican primary. Trump had just recently changed his residence from New York to Florida and declared Mar-a-Lago his primary residence, but a restriction in the sale of the resort years ago prevents it from being both a resort and a residence at the same time. "Trump agreed in writing years ago to change the use of the Mar-a-Lago property from a single-family residence to a private club owned by a corporation he controls." As long as it is a club, no one is allowed to stay there for more than seven days. Since it still now operates as a private club, it cannot be Trump's—or anyone else's—primary residence; Manuel Roig-Franzia, "Trump Made Florida His Official Residence. He May Have Also Made a Legal Mess," *Washington Post*, May 8, 2020, https://www.washingtonpost.com/lifestyle/style/trump-made -florida-his-official-residence-he-may-have-also-made-a-legal-mess/ 2020/05/07/17d53fb2-849c-11ea-878a-86477a724bdb_story.html.

14. Ed Pilkington, "Crystal Mason Begins Prison Sentence in Texas for Crime of Voting," *Guardian*, September 28, 2018, https://www.theguardian.com/us-news/2018/sep/28/crystal-mason -begins-prison-sentence-in-texas-for-of-voting.

15. Though, of course, the history of the struggle for voting and civil rights in the U.S. is one of great struggle at great personal risk. The account here describes Republicans' thinking and calculation, not the likely responses from minoritized communities, given their history. In any case, staying home need not mean not voting, since many states do offer the opportunity to vote by mail, and the coronavirus pandemic is increasing the

availability of that option. In this context, we can see better why Trump and the Republican Party now decry voting by mail, because it can be done from home. In addition to castigating states that provide mail-in voting, Trump has also proclaimed his intention to defund the U.S. Postal Service, which, some point out, may be another way to curb voting by mail; Grace Panetta, "Trump Reportedly Rejected Approving a Bailout Package That Would Rescue the US Postal Service, and It Could Be a Disaster for States Trying to Expand Voting by Mail," *Business Insider*, April 12, 2020, https://www.businessinsider.com/postal-service -funding-crisis-could-harm-voting-by-mail-coronavirus-2020-4, and Paul Waldman, "Trump's War on the Postal Service Just Got a Giant Boost," *Washington Post*, May 7, 2020, https://www. washingtonpost.com/opinions/2020/05/07/trumps-war-postal -service-just-got-giant-boost/.

16. Trump, "Donald J. Trump, "Remarks by President Trump in a Meeting with Governor Hutchinson of Arkansas and Governor Kelly of Kansas."

27. Loose Threads

1. Homer, *The Odyssey*, trans. Emily Wilson (New York: W. W. Norton, 2017).

2. Emily Wilson, "Introduction," in Homer, *The Odyssey*, 45. It is worth noting, though, that Odysseus's raft may have been designed to be permanent, but it crashes and is broken up by the sea.

3. But, then, just like *Gaslight*'s Anton, so, too, the men in Penelope's palace enlist the household's women to their own nefarious purpose, and the women, Penelope's servants, betray her. They reveal the secret of her unraveling, and Penelope, discovered, is finally forced to finish the fabric, "perforce." Penelope also uses other wiles, as the suitors know. For example, she is said to pass notes to some of her admirers, then to position herself just out of reach. *Gaslight*, directed by George Cukor (MGM, 1944), DVD.

4. As some point out, when Odysseus finally returns, and Penelope does not recognize him, it is unclear whether that is

an unwitting failure of recognition or itself also a canny, willful defense of her now accustomed independence.

5. The "true goal of totalitarian propaganda is not persuasion, but organization of the polity. . . . What convinces masses are not facts, and not even invented facts, but only the consistency of the system of which they are presumably part," says Hannah Arendt in *The Origins of Totalitarianism*, suggesting the radicality of the loose thread in opposing such systems; Arendt, *The Origins of Totalitarianism* (New York: Harcourt, Brace, Jovanovich, 1973), 361.

6. Carol Dougherty, Chapter 5, "'Come Brother. Let's Go Home': Restorative Nostalgia in Toni Morrison's *Home*," in *Travel and Home in Homer's Odyssey and Contemporary Literature: Critical Encounters and Nostalgic Returns* (Oxford: Oxford University Press, 2019), 155. See also the excellent piece by Susan Neal Mayberry, "*Home* as a Rosetta Stone for Toni Morrison's Decryptions of the Masculine," in *US-China Foreign Language* 15, no. 5 (May 2017): 315–29.

7. As Dougherty also notes, Morrison made clear *Home* was an exploration of the *Odyssey*, and there are several connections between the two that have the power to alter our readings of both. Notably Morrison's Odysseus character, Frank, has the middle nickname "Smart." Like the famously canny Odysseus, Frank is a trickster. See Toni Morrison, *Home* (New York: Vintage International, 2013).

8. Dougherty says, "Since Achilles died on the battlefield, the *Iliad* never even tries to imagine his homecoming, and the *Odyssey* . . . tends to downplay the disruptive level of violence that Odysseus brings into the home as well as any difficulties that Odysseus might have in making the transition from the battlefield to the home front."

9. There are two Hegelianisms in the novel. The brother-sister relation, which is assumed to be non-erotic, and the turn to burial as a humanizing practice; see Bonnie Honig, *Antigone, Interrupted* (Cambridge: Cambridge University Press, 2013) for further discussion of both in the context of Sophocles's *Antigone*.

10. I discuss the politics of the AIDS quilt in Honig, *Antigone, Interrupted*.

11. "Nothing human is perfect," observes Hannah Arendt about the "holes of oblivion" constructed by the Nazis to disappear any evidence of human goodness or resistance to their program. "Nothing human is perfect, and there are simply too many people in the world to make oblivion possible. One man will always be left alive to tell the story." He will be a loose thread. Erin Overbey, "Eighty-Five from the Archive: Hannah Arendt," *New Yorker*, April 29, 2010, https://www.newyorker.com/books/double-take/eighty-five-from-the-archive-hannah-arendt.

12. Wilson, "Introduction."

13. *Gaslight*, directed by George Cukor (MGM, 1944), DVD.

14. Notably, when a woman in Russia was in the fall of 2020 unexpectedly elected mayor of her small city (she was a cleaner in the town hall and ran as part of a corrupt plot to re-elect the current mayor), her "first order of business—after finding her replacement as cleaner, that is—she plans to bring streetlights to the village, she said, something that people have long been asking for." Streetlights. What a radical notion. (https://www.nytimes.com/2020/10/24/world/europe/russia-election-mayor.html).

15. *The Sixth Sense*, directed by M. Night Shyamalan, (Hollywood Pictures, 1999).

16. Angelique M. Davis and Rose Ernst, "Racial Gaslighting," *Politics, Groups, and Identities* 7, no. 4 (2019): 761–74.

Credits

An earlier version of Chapter 3 was published as "The President's House Is Empty," *Boston Review*, January 19, 2017, http://bostonreview.net/politics/bonnie-honig-president -house-empty.

An earlier version of Chapter 4 was published as "He Said, He Said: The Feminization of James Comey," *Boston Review*, June 10, 2017, http://bostonreview.net/politics-gender -sexuality/bonnie-honig-he-said-he-said-feminization -james-comey.

An earlier version of Chapter 5 was published as "What White Supremacists Want," *Boston Review*, September 25, 2017, http://bostonreview.net/politics/bonnie-honig-mem bers-only-president.

An earlier version of Chapter 6 was published as "An Empire unto Himself," *Boston Review*, October 13, 2017, http://bostonreview.net/politics/bonnie-honig-empire -unto-himself.

Earlier versions of Chapter 7 were published as "(Un)Reality TV: Trump, Kelly, and the Revolving Door of

Whiteness," *The Contemporary Condition*, October 23, 2017, http://contemporarycondition.blogspot.com/2017/10/unreality-tv-trump-kelly-and-revolving.html, and "Waiting for John Kelly?" *Politicsslashletters*, September 5, 2020, http://politicsslashletters.org/commentary/waiting-for-john-kelly/.

An earlier version of Chapter 8 was published as "Civility Is for Losers," *The Contemporary Condition*, June 27, 2018, http://contemporarycondition.blogspot.com/2018/06/civility-is-for-losers.html.

An earlier version of Chapter 9 was published as "'Entirely Consensual'? Stormy Daniels' #MeToo Moment," *Politicsslashletters*, March 27, 2018, http://politicsslashletters.org/commentary/entirely-consensual-stormy-daniels-metoo-moment/.

An earlier version of Chapter 10 was published as "The Trump Doctrine and the Gender Politics of Power," *Boston Review*, July 17, 2018, http://bostonreview.net/politics/bonnie-honig-trump-doctrine-and-gender-politics-power.

An earlier version of Chapter 11 was published as "A Thousand Points of Fight: Jon Stewart and the Limits of Mockery," *Los Angeles Review of Books*, July 31, 2018, https://blog.lareviewofbooks.org/essays/thousand-points-fight-jon-stewart-limits-mockery/.

An earlier version of Chapter 12 was published as "Trump's Presidency Is Not So 'Unprecedented' After All," *ABC Religion & Ethics*, September 12, 2018, https://www.abc.net.au/religion/american-politics-hasnt-changed-under-trump/10235820.

An earlier version of Chapter 13 was published as "Renovating the House (and Senate . . .)," *Los Angeles Review of Books*, September 9, 2018, http://blog.lareviewofbooks.org/essays/renovating-house-senate/.

Chapter 14 was previously published as "No Collision," *Boston Review*, December 10, 2018, http://bostonreview.net/science-nature-politics/bonnie-honig-no-collision.

An earlier version of Chapter 15 was co-published with Sara Rushing as "Epstein, Barr, and the Treatment of Civic Fatigue Syndrome," *The Contemporary Condition*, July 11, 2019, http://contemporarycondition.blogspot.com/2019/07/epstein-barr-and-treatment-of-civic.html.

An earlier version of Chapter 16 was published as "Mueller, They Wrote," *Politicsslashletters*, July 25, 2019, http://politicsslashletters.org/uncategorized/mueller-they-wrote/.

Chapter 17 was previously published anonymously as "'Unbelievable': Scenes from a Structure," *Politicsslashletters*, September 21, 2019, http://politicsslashletters.org/uncatego rized/unbelievable-scenes-from-a-structure/.

An earlier version of Chapter 19 was published as "Breathing Room: Dingell v. Trump," *Politicsslashletters*, December 21, 2019, http://politicsslashletters.org/uncategorized/breathing-room-dingell-v-trump/.

An earlier version of Chapter 20 was published as "Rambo Politics from Reagan to Trump," *Boston Review*, January 7, 2020, http://bostonreview.net/war-security-politics/bonnie-honig-rambo-politics-reagan-trump.

Chapter 21 is a revised excerpt of "*12 Angry Men*: Care for the Agon and the Varieties of Masculine Experience," *Theory & Event* 22, no. 3 (July 2019): 701–16.

Chapter 22 was previously published as "In the Streets a Serenade," *Politicsslashletters*, March 14, 2020, http://politics slashletters.org/uncategorized/in-the-streets-a-serenade/.

An earlier version of Chapter 23 was published as "Spitballing in a Pandemic," *Politicsslashletters*, April 25, 2020, http://politicsslashletters.org/commentary/spitballing-in -a-pandemic/.

An earlier version of Chapter 24 was published as "Build That Wall: The Politics of Motherhood in Portland," *The Contemporary Condition*, July 22, 2020, http://contemporary condition.blogspot.com/2020/07/build-that-wall-politics-of -motherhood.html.

An earlier version of Chapter 25 was published as "The 14th Amendment: Bigotry's Latest Casualty," *Los Angeles Review of Books*, November 1, 2018, https://blog.lareviewof books.org/essays/14th-amendment-bigotrys-latest-casualty/.

Earlier versions of Chapter 26 were published as "The People Want Their House Back," *The Contemporary Condition*, at http://contemporarycondition.blogspot.com/2020/ 08/the-people-want-their-house-back.html, and as "The White House Has Become Trump's House," at https://blogs .lse.ac.uk/usappblog/2020/09/04/the-white-house-has -become-trumps-house/#Author.

The still from *Gaslight* (p. 19) appears courtesy of the Everett Collection of Newark, New Jersey. The still from *Stranger Things* (p. 26) appears courtesy of Netflix/Photofest © Netflix. The still from *Veep* (p. 57) appears courtesy of HBO/Photofest © HBO. I am grateful to Luiz C. Ribeiro for permission to reproduce the photograph of protesters carry- ing pictures of Jeffrey Epstein and Donald Trump (p. 109) and to Al Drago for permission to reproduce the photograph of Donald Trump during a White House briefing (p. 159). The photograph of Portland's "Naked Athena" (p. 167) appears courtesy of Reuters and Nathan Howard. Dora Wheeler 1886 silk embroidery, *Penelope Unraveling Her Work at Night* (p. 189) appears courtesy of the Metropolitan Museum of Art © The Metropolitan Museum of Art, image source: Art Resource, New York.

Bonnie Honig is Nancy Duke Lewis Professor of Modern Culture and Media (MCM) and Political Science at Brown University. Her most recent books are *Public Things: Democracy in Disrepair* and *A Feminist Theory of Refusal*.